COYOTE THE TRICKSTER

Among the rich and ancient legends of the
North American Indians, there are many
stories about a supernatural being called the
Trickster–a creature endowed by the Indian
myth-maker with a many-sided personality.
In one story he is foolish enough to get into
trouble with a magical rock, but tricky
enough to get out of the difficulty; in another,
he appears as a supernatural hero doing
mighty battle, but using trickery as well as
power to win . . . Two distinguished Cana-
dian poets combine expert story-telling with
a wise and witty reflection of human nature
in exploiting the riches of a notable and
unusual range of folk material.

COYOTE
THE TRICKSTER

Legends of the North American Indians

Retold by

GAIL ROBINSON
AND
DOUGLAS HILL

Illustrated by
GRAHAM McCALLUM

CRANE RUSSAK · NEW YORK

Published in the United States in 1976 by
Crane, Russak & Company, Inc.
347 Madison Avenue
New York, N.Y. 10017

ISBN 0-8448-0923-3
LC 76-7248

Printed in the United States of America

Contents

Introduction

AMONG the rich and ancient legends of the North American Indians are many stories about a character called the Trickster.

He was a supernatural being, one of a race of powerful beings who most usually appeared in the form of animals, though they could take human form if they wished. Each of these animal gods seemed to have an especially large measure of the abilities, and general behaviour, of his particular animal species. So it was that the animal-god Bear was noted for his strength, as ordinary bears are; the animal-god Beaver was a water being and a practical, hard-working soul; and the animal-god Deer seemed sensitive and nervous.

The Trickster animal-god comes from a particularly clever and mischievous sort of animal — though different Indian tribes have different Tricksters. The Trickster of the Great Plains tribes is the animal-god Coyote, and he is found also in the tales of tribes from the south-western deserts and mountains of America, and from California. The Indians and some Eskimos of the north Pacific coast have a Trickster called Raven; in other tribes' myths the Trickster may be Hare, or Mink, or Bluejay, or Fox.

Some Indian tribes call their animal gods the 'First People' or, more simply, 'the People' — and we have taken this name for them and used it in all the stories in this book, so as not to be confusing. They were the First People because they lived, the myths say, at a time when the world was freshly made, and when they and the animals were the only living beings. But they were also still there when mankind finally came small and naked and ignorant into the world.

A few myths say that it was that special animal god, the

5

Trickster, who brought the first human beings into life. Other tales say that humans were created by a greater Being, and that the Trickster and the other People merely shared the world with them for a while. Sometimes the Trickster looked after the humans, and taught them things so that they would not always be naked and ignorant. From the Trickster, then, mankind received the great gifts of fire and corn, and learned the arts of pottery and weapon-making.

But the Trickster was not always a hero or a kindly god. The old tales also show him making a comic fool of himself, getting into trouble because of his greed or curiosity or pride or sheer stupidity. And, more than anything else, as his name shows, he was a mischievous and crafty being who loved playing tricks on others. Often, when his foolishness would get him into trouble, his trickery and wiliness would get him out. Even his more heroic deeds would sometimes grow out of sly and deceitful tricks that he set out to play on his fellow creatures.

So the Trickster, whether he is Coyote or Raven or one of the other animal gods, is many different kinds of character wrapped up in one — a silly fool and a splendid hero, a god-like gift-bringer and a trouble-making practical joker. And because of this he seems very *human*. His stories reminded the Indians, and can remind us, that ordinary people as well as the People can be stupid and clever, cruel and kind, brave and foolish all at the same time.

I

Coyote Steals a Blanket

UTE

IN the time before man had come on to the earth, Coyote was wandering through the mountains admiring their height and the sharpness of their peaks. Along a narrow canyon he came upon the house of another of the People, Hummingbird. Coyote stayed with him overnight and was made welcome, and in the morning Hummingbird asked where Coyote was going.

'I am just wandering,' said Coyote. 'Today I will go farther along this canyon and see what is at its end. Tomorrow, who knows?'

'There is nothing farther along this canyon,' said Hummingbird, 'nothing to see and no water. You should go along that ridge instead.' He pointed to a high slope at one side of the canyon. 'It will lead you to water, and will also lead to the top of the highest mountain, from which you can see over almost the whole world.'

'No,' said Coyote, 'that sounds interesting, but I want to go along this canyon. I can do without water for a day or two.'

'Don't be foolish,' said Hummingbird. 'Take my advice and follow that ridge. It is a much better route.'

Coyote thought it was odd that Hummingbird should try so hard to keep him from exploring the canyon. And so, because he was Coyote, he became both very stubborn and very curious. Nothing Hummingbird could say would make him change his mind.

Finally Hummingbird gave up. 'All right,' he said, 'go your own way, do as you wish.'

'I will,' said Coyote. 'I always do. But now will you tell me why you try to keep me out of this canyon?'

'There is something very dangerous up ahead,' said

9

Hummingbird. 'If you go that way, you will likely get into serious trouble. You always do that, too.'

'What is this dangerous thing?' asked Coyote.

'Never mind that,' said Hummingbird. 'Just pay attention. Along the canyon you will come to an open gully filled with large rocks. On the rocks you will see many brightly coloured blankets. It may seem strange to you, that so many good blankets should be lying on rocks out in the wilderness. But no matter how odd it seems, do not take any of the blankets, do not even touch them.'

'Why not?' asked Coyote. 'What will happen?'

Hummingbird shook his head. 'If you leave the blankets alone, nothing will happen. You can be a fool sometimes, Coyote, but if you are a fool this time you will lose your life. For once, listen to good advice and follow it.'

And no matter how Coyote pestered him, Hummingbird would say no more about the blankets — except to repeat, over and over, that it was time Coyote learned to do as he was told by people who knew better.

Finally Coyote turned his back on Hummingbird and went on his way down the canyon, highly curious about this strange new sight. Soon he came to the place where the canyon opened into a wide gully strewn with great boulders. On several of them, as Hummingbird had said, were large, bright, heavy blankets.

Coyote skulked round the edges of the gully, sniffing the air, cocking his ears, peering this way and that. But he saw and heard and smelt nothing but the mountain wind, the hard earth, a few straggling bunches of dry grass, the huge rocks and the colour-splashes made by the blankets.

'Whatever the dangerous thing is,' he thought to himself, 'it seems to be away from here at the moment. So I can quickly take a closer look at all this.'

Moving as silently as dust, he slipped up to the nearest rock and reached out to feel the blanket. It was richly and beautifully woven, as thick as the fur of a bear.

10

'Why, these are wonderful blankets,' thought Coyote. 'How foolish it is to let such fine things lie around in the mountains, where they can do no good.'

Again he went to the edge of the gully and hunted around it. Again there was no sign of danger of any kind.

'That Hummingbird talks like a foolish old woman,' thought Coyote. 'I have touched a blanket and nothing has happened. I am sure nothing would happen if I took one. And the nights are cold in the mountains. It would be pleasant to have a warm blanket round me tonight.'

His eye had been caught by one especially splendid red blanket, lying on top of the most immense rock of all, at least twice Coyote's height. He went to the rock, leaped up, grasped one corner of the red blanket and whisked it down off the rock. Then he crouched beside the rock, perfectly still. But no sound or scent or sight of danger appeared.

Laughing to himself, Coyote stood up and put the blanket around him. It was soft and heavy and wonderfully warm, and he felt that the colour suited him. So he rolled it up, put it over his shoulder and leaped to the edge of the gully. Still there was no sign of anything that might be a danger. So, singing happily, and now and then reaching up to stroke the softness of his new blanket, Coyote went on his way.

The way led to a long, gravelly slope that finally levelled out on to the floor of a valley. There grass and meadow flowers grew, and patches of trees, fed by a little stream combed clean in its gravel bed. So Coyote knew that Hummingbird had lied about the lack of water, just to keep him away from the blankets.

'He probably wanted all the blankets for himself,' thought Coyote. 'It is as well that I am not easily frightened.' Feeling proud of himself, he bent over the stream for a refreshing drink. As he stood up, he glanced back the way he had come.

11

High on the gravel slope above the valley there was a large cloud of dust rising, as if dragged up by a gusty, spinning whirl of wind.

Coyote moved unhurriedly to a slight rise on the valley floor, and looked again. The dust cloud was closer now, and even larger. Straining his eyes, Coyote could make out a vast shape at the centre of the cloud.

It looked like an enormous rock.

Coyote rubbed his eyes, and looked again. Without doubt, the cloud of dust was being thrown up by an immense rock rolling speedily down the slope.

It looked very much like the rock from which Coyote had taken the red blanket.

Coyote began to feel somewhat nervous. He set off at a rapid trot across the valley towards the next range of mountains that rose hazily in the distance. As he neared the mountains, he slowed his pace and looked back again.

The rock was still rolling. It had reached the valley floor, and was nearly at the rise where Coyote had previously been standing. As he watched, the rock began to roll up the rise. Its movement slowed as it climbed, until it was only creeping along. Finally, just before reaching the top of the rise, it stopped.

Coyote laughed, feeling much safer. Clearly the rock could not catch him if it could not roll all the way up steep slopes. He turned away, but then just to be sure glanced back once more.

He was horrified to see that the rock had resumed its rolling. It must have stopped only for an instant, to gather itself. Now it was over the top of the rise, and was rolling with gathering speed down the slope towards Coyote. It was coming so fast that he could make out the markings on its surface, the huge granite creases and cracks and lumps and jagged chipped edges.

Coyote was suddenly very frightened. Clutching the blanket firmly, he turned and fled towards the mountains.

At the foot of the nearest mountain, without pausing, he sprang up its side. By the time he reached the top his chest ached from the great gasping breaths he was taking, and his legs shook and trembled from his efforts. He looked down, and there was the rock rolling slowly up the lower fringes of the mountain.

Again it stopped as the incline grew steeper. Then it began to roll again, but in a zig-zag path — going sideways along the mountainside, and upwards at an angle that was not too steep, then turning and going sideways and upwards in the other direction. So it came nearer and nearer to the peak where Coyote sat, regaining his breath.

'Since it is climbing so slowly,' thought Coyote, 'I might be able to give it a push and roll it back down the mountain. Then it might give up and leave me alone.'

So he crept down towards the huge rock, which by then was lurching along no faster than a tortoise. But as Coyote moved near, the boulder suddenly hurled itself forward, directly at him.

Only Coyote's sure-footed speed saved him. He dodged aside as the rock crashed down on the spot where he had been standing. Instantly the rock lunged at him again; and that time, as Coyote dodged, he felt the cold stone graze his leg.

Yelping with fear, Coyote turned and rushed again up the mountain, over the top and down the other side. At the foot of the mountain he looked back. The rock was rumbling along after him with terrible speed.

Ahead Coyote saw a wide ravine. Reaching its edge he sprang up and out as far as he could, and just reached the other side, scrambling for a foothold in loose earth. Behind him the rock was rolling at the lip of the ravine, and Coyote hoped that it would stop, or fall in. It did neither. It struck a smaller rock half buried in the earth, bounced high in the air, sailed across the ravine and landed on the other side with a crunch that rattled the highest crags.

13

Coyote howled, and ran on. Next he came to a pair of towering cliffs, and a narrow pass between them that was hardly more than a crack. Coyote plunged into it, gasping with relief for he knew that the rock was too large to follow him through the gap. He loped slowly away, his strength returning as his fear and exhaustion faded. Soon he emerged from the other end of the pass into the open.

Coyote was feeling pleased with himself at his escape when his eye caught a flicker of motion to one side. He turned, and there was the rock, rolling towards him. It had clearly come the long way round the cliffs. Coyote's knees felt watery and he whimpered as, again, he fled the great bulk that was seeking to crush him as he would crush a beetle.

But this time, as he ran, a new idea came to him. 'My friend Deer lives near this place,' he thought. 'Perhaps he will help me — or at least perhaps the rock will turn to chasing him instead.'

Soon he came to the high meadow where the Deer lived. 'Help!' shouted Coyote. 'Deer, my friend! Help me!'

Deer came out of his house and stared. Then he bounded to Coyote's side and ran along with him, looked back in wonder at the giant rock rolling frightfully along behind them.

'This rock is trying to kill me,' gasped Coyote. 'I can do nothing against it, and I am so tired that soon it will catch me and crush me to death. Only your powerful antlers, my friend, can bring it to a halt.'

At these flattering remarks Deer felt very pleased and proud. He raised his great head and shook his ten-pronged antlers. 'As you say,' he told Coyote, 'only someone as strong as I can stop this rock. Now watch me.'

And he turned, lowered his head and bounded towards the rock, the muscles of his great neck firm as an elm tree trunk. His antlers struck the vast rock exactly in its centre.

The rock's pace slowed slightly, only for an instant. But

14

the topmost prongs of Deer's antlers snapped off like dead cedar twigs, and Deer was flung to one side, to lie groaning with pain and shock.

The rock then seemed to pick up speed, and thundered across the meadow towards Coyote. Again Coyote began to run — and again an idea came to him, lending some new strength to his stumbling legs.

'My friend Mountain Sheep lives on a high place near here,' he thought. 'I will seek his help.'

After much climbing, Coyote reached the clearing on the cliff-top home of Mountain Sheep, a mighty curly-horned ram as old as the mountains themselves. The climb had left the rock far behind, and Mountain Sheep, seeing only Coyote looking exhausted and terrified, asked in some surprise what was the matter. Between gasps for breath, Coyote explained his danger. But he was careful not to mention Deer's failure to stop the rock.

'I can do nothing against this thing,' moaned Coyote. 'Only someone as large and powerful as yourself could hope to oppose it. Will you use your mighty horns to save me?'

But Mountain Sheep was somewhat shrewder than Deer. 'I may help you,' said he. 'First tell me why this rock is pursuing you. Could it be because of that beautiful new blanket that you are holding so tightly?'

At first Coyote pretended that he did not know why the rock was chasing him. But he knew there was no time to waste, and when Mountain Sheep insisted, he finally told the truth about the blanket.

'Then you need no help from me,' said Mountain Sheep. 'Give the blanket back to the rock and it will leave you alone.'

Coyote clutched the blanket to his chest. 'No! I like this blanket — it is mine now! I will not give it back!'

Mountain Sheep shrugged. 'Why should I help you, then, if you persist in this foolishness?' Then a sly look came over his face. 'Of course, if you were willing to give *me* the

15

blanket, I might change my mind.'

But Mountain Sheep was no match for Coyote in slyness. Coyote thought for a moment, then said, 'I would be willing to share the blanket, so you could use it for part of the time.'

'That will not do,' said Mountain Sheep. 'If I am to help you, it must be mine.'

'That it will never be,' said Coyote. 'If you will help me, you may have a share in the blanket. If you will not, I will give it back to the rock and you will have *none* of it.'

Mountain Sheep could see that it was better to have a share in the blanket than none at all, but he felt that somehow he had got the worst of the bargain. Still, he agreed. And as he did so, the rock, which had kept on coming in its tireless way, rolled up on to the cliff-top where they stood.

Mountain Sheep lowered his head, thrusting forward his forehead — itself granite-hard — and his immense curling horns. Then he plunged towards the rock at a gallop. The front curve of his horns struck the rock in its exact centre.

The impact jolted the rock, and Coyote could see that a small sliver of stone, about the size of a leaf, had been chipped from its surface by Mountain Sheep's charge. But Sheep himself had bounced back away from the rock as if he were a rubber ball, and was standing on quivering legs that finally gave way to let him fall slowly into a heap. He was still breathing, Coyote saw, but he was completely stunned. And the rock was still rolling.

For a moment, as it towered over him, Coyote felt that he might after all give up the blanket. But the mere thought of losing its rich warmth put strength into him, and once more he turned and ran.

Ahead he saw a long, sweeping ridge that rose and rose impossibly, until it reached the underside of the clouds and vanished from view. Coyote began to climb it, and the rock followed, slowly as always when it was mounting an incline.

But Coyote knew that it would always follow him, that however far ahead of it or above it he went, it would still keep coming until he, or it, was destroyed.

As he was thinking these gloomy thoughts, he was moving higher and higher on the great ridge — until finally he realized that he could see for an immense distance. It seemed as if almost the entire world was spread out below him.

Then he knew where he was, for he remembered Hummingbird telling him about the tallest mountain of all, that rose somewhere near Hummingbird's home. Once again an idea came to Coyote, and he moved off the ridge and along the mountainside, seeking a way down to the little canyon where all the trouble had first begun.

Shortly he had descended the mountain and was back at the house of Hummingbird, who looked at him with disdain.

'So you have done just what I warned you not to do,' said Hummingbird.

'You might have told me that I would be pursued forever by a killer rock,' snarled Coyote.

'Would it have stopped you stealing the blanket?' asked Hummingbird. 'You would not have believed me, and would have got into trouble just the same.'

Coyote saw the truth in this, and so did not answer Hummingbird. Instead he said, 'Will you help me anyway, friend? You know all about this rock, so you must know how to stop it.'

'Certainly,' said Hummingbird. 'Give back its blanket.'

'I have run far with this blanket,' said Coyote. 'My chest aches, my legs scream with pain, my feet are torn raw from the rocks. Two of my friends lie bruised and damaged in the mountains. And all because of this blanket. Yet it is mine now, and I will not give it up.'

'Then I cannot help you,' said Hummingbird.

'Very well,' said Coyote. 'I will wait here until the rock comes, and you will be able to watch as it rolls over

17

me and crushes me to death.'

Hummingbird sighed. 'There is a spirit in that rock,' he said. 'A powerful old spirit of the mountain peaks. It has no real mind, not like we of the People. Yet it is alive, and durable and hard as the stone itself. I may be able to oppose it, but I may not. I do not know why I should risk myself for a greedy fool who will not listen to good sense.'

Coyote said nothing. After a moment Hummingbird sighed again and said, 'Very well. I will try. It is not right that one of the People — even you — should be destroyed.'

Coyote smiled and bowed. As he did so there was a crunch of gravel, and the great rock loomed into sight round a bend in the canyon.

Hummingbird flung himself into the air. His wings whirred with such astounding speed that no eye could see their motion. He darted down at the great rock, flitting aside at the last instant before collision. And the rock slid to a stop, gouging a huge furrow in the ground.

Again Hummingbird dived at it, his wingbeats making a deep organ hum in the air. The rock groaned and quivered, shaking the earth.

A third time Hummingbird flew at it, and the sound of his wings rose to a vibrant howl that made Coyote cover his ears in pain.

And the vast rock cracked across, and fell apart in two halves like a clam shell dropped by a gull.

Over the sound of Hummingbird's wings there rose an eerie, high-pitched, raging shriek that climbed towards the mountain peaks, and faded, and died away.

Hummingbird stood wearily before Coyote. 'Now the rock is mere stone again, and I am very tired and sad that all this should have happened. And no doubt you will go on doing as you please and paying no heed to advice and making others get you out of trouble.'

'I expect so,' agreed Coyote. 'I always do as I please. But thank you, anyway. I shall rest very comfortably in my

18

warm new blanket, after all the running about I have done today.'

And he went on his way, laughing to himself.

Coyote and Brown Giant

NAVAHO

JUST after the time when the lakes, mountains and rivers had taken their places as we know them now, a great fear came to the animal gods who called themselves the People. A destroyer had come among them, a mighty giant who made his home in a cave overlooking the only path through the mountains, and who caught and killed any travellers who passed along that way. The giant was said to be entirely the brown colour of the earth when it was wet. He was a powerful god from a time beyond all imagination, a time even before the People themselves had come into the world.

One evening all the People gathered, in the shadowed protection of the deepest canyon, to decide what to do about the terror in the mountains.

'Once I flew high against the red eye of the sun,' said Sparrowhawk, 'to see the brown giant. Even then he frightened me, for he is nearly as large as a mountain himself.'

'I crept through the long grasses to look at him,' whispered Mouse, 'and saw gnawed bones piled as high as a tree outside his cave.'

'Once the giant stamped into the forest where I live,' said Weasel, 'and tore up a huge fir tree twice the thickness of my body. Now he uses it as a club to crush the skulls of his victims.'

'What can we do about the giant?' Skunk asked. 'Surely he must be killed. But which among us will go into the mountains and do this task?'

All the people at the meeting looked at each other, but in the eyes of each of them — even Black Bear, humped and massive as a granite boulder — there was the fearful

23

knowledge that the brown god's strength was too great.

Mountain Sheep broke the silence that had come over the meeting. 'It is clear that none of us is strong enough to battle the giant. Perhaps all of us together would not be strong enough, for none of us know the limits of his power. But remember that no strength, however great, can withstand great cleverness and deep cunning. Who among us is the most clever and cunning?'

'Coyote!' said Woodpecker instantly. And all the others took up her cry — 'Coyote!' 'Where is Coyote?'

Coyote was not at the meeting, they found. But Elk and some of the others remembered seeing him in the earliest days of the spring sun's warmth, when he told them he was on his way across the mountains and down to the sea.

'He is too foot-loose, always off on his journeys,' grumbled Spider, 'never here when he is needed.'

'We will send him a message,' Mountain Sheep said. 'Some of us can take it to the sea, and search for him. If he is not there, we will look through the whole world to find him.'

So the People took a stone and put on it their special markings that would speak to Coyote of trouble and danger and their need for his help. Wild Goose took the stone and rose with it high over the crags, where the forests on the mountainsides looked as small as tufts of grass, and where he would be hidden from even the giant's gaze. When he grew weary he let the stone drop into a rushing river. There Salmon dived to retrieve it from the murky bottom where the sun's hot gaze had never reached. Downstream Salmon flung himself with all his speed, the river's current hurling him along, faster and faster, until he came to the place where the river grew flat and wide as a lake as it made ready to lose itself in the sea. Then Salmon leaped high out of the water and flung the stone into the air where Gull came to catch it. For many days Gull flew tirelessly along the empty strands of the sea — until the day came when he saw Coyote lying on a flat rock in the sun.

Gull descended and gave Coyote the message stone.

'So the People call to me when they are in trouble,' said Coyote, to tease Gull. 'Is there none among them with the strength or courage to save them now?'

'There are many!' Gull said angrily. 'But it is your craft and slyness that is needed now, not strength nor courage.'

'Indeed,' Coyote laughed. 'Then tell all the strong, brave People that I will come soon and face this danger for them.'

At that Gull became so angry that he opened his wings and flew rapidly away out to sea, without telling Coyote any more about the nature of the danger. Still smiling, Coyote rose from his sunny rock, stretched, and began his journey inland to join the People, where he assumed he would find out what he needed to know. So it was that, unprepared, he took a pass through the mountains that would lead him to the lair of the brown giant.

Eventually he entered the giant's valley, running easily along the rocky trail. As he got farther in, he noticed how still and quiet the valley had become. There seemed to be no living creatures in the wilderness around him — no blue-jays or squirrels in the trees, no snake trails along the ledges, not even mosquitoes hovering in the sunbeams. The eerie silence caused Coyote to move more carefully, making no sound of his own. Then all at once he stopped short, sniffing the air. The breeze bore upon it an odour of blood and death.

'This must be the danger the People spoke of,' Coyote thought. 'What kind of creature has come among us?'

Cautiously he left the trail, slipping like a grey shadow along the mountainside towards the source of the stench. In this way he came upon the open black throat of a cave, and saw outside it an immense mound of bones. Coyote stared at the bones, recognizing among them the great horned skull of the mountain sheep, the delicate ribs of antelope, even here and there the sturdy leg bones of the cougar.

As Coyote gazed, chilled, at the cave mouth, he felt the sun suddenly leave his back, heard behind him the faintest grind of rock against rock, and heard above him a whistling of something moving at speed through the air. As Coyote sprang to one side, the rock where he had been standing was smashed to gravel by a blow from an enormous club.

Coyote leaped away up the mountainside, looking back over his shoulder with astonishment. He saw that the club was fashioned from a huge pine tree, and that it was held lightly in the hand of a giant, all in brown, whose head stretched up nearly to the clouds.

'Do not run, little creature,' rumbled the giant in a voice like the crashing of a waterfall. 'You will not escape me.'

Coyote stopped and turned boldly. 'I am not trying to escape you, giant,' he said. 'I have heard that you are the mightiest being in this world, and I have come to serve you.'

'Serve me?' the giant said, and his laughter boomed like a mountain snowslide in winter. 'How can a spindly little thing like you serve me?'

'I can help you catch your food,' Coyote said. 'I can run the fastest and leap the farthest of any being in the mountains; no one's nose is keener, no foot is more silent. I can drive other creatures towards you so that you need never leave the comfort of your home. And if any of them should dodge your club – as, remember, I have done – I will pursue them and drive them back again.'

'Good,' the giant said. 'You are very quick, as you say. Perhaps you can be of use to me. And if not – then I will always have you nearby, to eat when I please.'

So the giant took Coyote down the mountain and into his cave. The floor of the cave was littered with more bones, smelling as vilely as those outside. Filth of all kinds was strewn or heaped around the cave, and in one corner was a ragged heap of foul skins that was the giant's sleeping-place.

'What a beautiful house you have!' Coyote cried. 'It is clear that you are a giant who knows all about comfort, and beauty, and enjoyment.'

The giant was delighted at the flattery. 'You are right, little creature,' he boasted. 'No one in the world knows more about those things than I do.'

'Perhaps you will teach me about such things,' Coyote went on, 'while I am your servant. To begin with, please tell me — because I am too stupid to see for myself — why you have placed your sweat-house so far from this cave.'

'Sweat-house?' the giant rumbled. 'I have no sweat-house.'

'Have you not?' said Coyote, who knew it perfectly well. 'How could a master of comfort and pleasure such as yourself have overlooked it? Why, there is no enjoyment in the world as great as that of sitting peacefully in the hot darkness of a sweat-house. Doing so makes one cleaner than ever before, without any effort. It makes one healthy, getting rid of many poisons and evils from the fat beneath the skin. And of course the sweat-house is the best place to work certain kinds of changes.'

'Changes?' said the giant. 'What changes?'

'Magical ones,' Coyote said, pretending modesty. 'They call me Coyote the Changer, and I work my best changing magic inside a sweat-house. Why, it was there that I made myself into the fastest runner in the world. I could show you how to do that, if you like, and then you too could run like the mountain wind, and you would not need me to pursue your food for you.'

'That would be a good change,' said the giant, 'if it could be done. Yes, show it to me.'

'First I must show you how to build the sweat-house,' Coyote said.

So the giant began to build, following Coyote's instructions. Coyote told him how to use three forked poles as the frame of the house, and the giant wrenched up three tall pines, tore off their tops and roots and plunged them deep into the ground, locked together at the top. Then Coyote taught him to weave saplings and heavy branches around the framework, to form the walls, and then to pile turf up over the frame to make the sweat-house as nearly airtight as possible.

The giant laboured as he was told, and when he had heaped vast swathes of heavy turf on to the walls, the sweat-house was complete — save for a small opening at the very top of the cone-shape.

'The top must be covered,' Coyote said. 'Sweat-houses do not have smoke holes — they would let out the heat with the smoke.' And Coyote took a great slice of turf himself and sprang lightly up the side of the mountainous house to its very peak, where he closed off the last gap in the covering.

Then he and the giant made the special curtains for the doorway, sewing together the skins from the giant's sleeping-place, and arranging the curtains so that they hung across the door, overlapping one another like the waterproof feathers of a duck. Then Coyote sent the giant to collect special stones to hold the heat of the fire — stones, he said, with special mosses and lichens that would add to the power of the magical changes they would make.

'While you bring the stones,' Coyote said, 'I will gather the wood needed for the fire. It must be very dry and well-seasoned cedar, so that it will not smoke too much, and it should be from a tree struck by the lightning, so that some of its power will come into the sweat-house.'

So while the giant wrestled with boulders from the mountain, Coyote went into the forest and found a lightning-blasted cedar tree. Quickly he broke it up into smaller pieces he could carry, and took them back to the sweat-house.

But before he went inside, he picked up two long bones from the heap outside the giant's cave, and hid them at the bottom of the wood-pile.

At last all was ready, and the giant went into the huge house with Coyote, leaving the curtains folded back for light while Coyote quickly took coloured sand and laid out a sand painting around the place where the fire would be. Next he made two other sand paintings on the floor of the sweat-house, one small and one enormously large, at opposite sides of the house.

'The sand paintings gather and direct the power,' he told the giant. 'While we are performing the change we must remain within them — you within the large one, I within the small one.'

'Can we begin now?' the giant asked.

'Yes, now,' Coyote said. And he began to make fire, and build up a mighty blaze with the dry cedar wood. When the fire was going well, he closed the curtains of the sweat-house tight against the light and cool air from outside.

'Are you going to work the change now?' asked the giant impatiently.

'Not yet,' Coyote said. 'The fire must be fed and burn all of this wood, to gather the power.'

So, with the flames hurling their shadows against the thick walls of turf, and with the heat growing more and more intense so that the sweat began to pour from both their bodies, Coyote flung the cedar steadily on to the fire as it burned away. Slowly the pile of wood dwindled, until finally there were only a few sticks left — and beneath them the two long bones.

'Now,' he called to the giant, 'we will keep the rest of the sticks for later. You put on to the fire the stones you gathered, so they can grow hot and hold the heat of the fire. Then we will take our places in our sand paintings and begin the change.'

The giant hurried to bring to the fire the many immense

29

boulders that he had brought in, all of them thick with the mosses and lichens that Coyote had said were needed for the magic. Then the giant went quickly to his sand painting.

'Now remember that we cannot leave the paintings, or the power will not work,' Coyote said firmly.

'I remember,' the giant said.

'Then we can begin. Watch me closely,' Coyote said, 'for what I do now you will have to do afterwards.'

But of course the flames of the fire had already begun to burn the moss on the great stones, and heavy smoke was swirling through the sweat-house.

'I cannot see you very well,' the giant complained, 'so how am I to watch what you do? The house is filling with smoke, sweat is running into my eyes and you are so small and so far away from me. What is happening?'

'All is well,' Coyote answered him. By then his own eyes were smarting from the thickening smoke, and he could no longer see the giant — which meant that the giant could certainly not see Coyote. 'I will simply *tell* you what I am doing, and then you can do the same in your turn.'

'Begin, then,' the giant grumbled impatiently.

'You will remember,' Coyote said, 'that this change is to make you able to run like the mountain wind. So naturally the change must happen to your legs. What I did to make myself the fastest runner in the world was to cut off my legs, and then grow new ones with a special power in them.'

'Cut off your legs?' the giant growled, suspicion in his voice. 'I don't believe that. How do I know my legs will grow again, if I cut them off?'

'I will show you,' Coyote said. 'I will cut mine off again, and grow new ones, so that you will not worry. See, first I take my knife and cut down through my legs till I reach the bone. Then I cut the flesh away, take the bone in my hands, and break it.'

'Wait,' shouted the giant, 'the smoke is thick and I can

see nothing of what you are doing!'

'Never mind,' Coyote said soothingly, 'I will reach out the bones of my leg and you can stretch out your hand and feel them, so you will be sure that I am not lying to you.'

Coyote picked up the two long bones he had hidden and reached out through the smoke towards the giant. The giant's vast brown arm stretched out, too, and his huge fingers touched the dry, clean bones.

'So it is true!' the giant marvelled. 'But did it not hurt you as you cut away your flesh?'

'A little,' Coyote replied, 'but you must put up with some pain in order to work this sort of change. And now I must finish the rest of it.'

And he took the two bones in his hands and broke them with a loud snap, then threw them on to the fire.

'Now my legs are off,' he cried, 'and already the new ones have begun to grow. Reach out again, brown giant, and you will see!'

Once again the giant stretched out his hand, and this time Coyote pushed his legs forward, so that the giant could touch them.

'They have grown back!' the giant said, awed. 'And will these legs be fast runners?'

'Even faster than the last ones,' Coyote assured him. 'Now it is your turn – think of how soon you will be running over the mountain-tops like the wind!'

'Like the wind!' the giant echoed. And Coyote caught a glimpse through the dense smoke of a knife flashing, and heard the giant groaning with pain, and then at last he heard two enormous cracks, as huge bones broke.

'I did not know it would hurt so much,' the giant moaned. 'When will my new legs come, and end the pain?'

Coyote went to stand over the legless body of the giant, lying on the floor of the sweat-house.

'You came to these mountains and brought pain and death to many beings, and many of my People,' he said grimly. 'Now Coyote has come, and has brought the same to you — pain, and death!'

And he picked up the giant's mighty club, and with all his strength swung it up, then down again on to the giant's skull. The sound of the blow echoed through the mountains as the giant rolled away, dead.

Thus Coyote made the mountains safe again for all creatures, and safe for the coming of humans.

3

Raven
and the Coming of Daylight

HAIDA

W<small>HEN</small> the earth was very young, it was dark and cold like a winter's night through all the year's seasons. Gull was the Custodian of Daylight, and he kept it locked tight in a cedar box beneath his wing. Being Custodian made Gull feel very important, and he was not going to lose his position by letting Daylight out of the box.

'He is too vain!' screeched Owl, at a meeting of the People upon Meeting Hill.

'We can never travel, in this darkness, to our half-homes in the south,' cried Robin. Her breast was bleached of colour for the lack of light.

'Even the dark mosses wither, and food is scarce,' whimpered Rabbit.

'One person is like another because I cannot map his face,' shouted Bear. 'Enemies pretend to be friends to share my blanket and bowl.'

'I cannot see my tail, to clean it of burrs,' whined Fox.

So all the People complained of Gull's arrogance and thoughtless self-importance.

Then Squirrel turned to Raven and said, 'Gull is your cousin. Perhaps he will listen to you. Perhaps you can tell him of your cold blood, and your blunderings in the darkness, and make him change his mind.'

So it was settled that Raven should meet Gull on Meeting Hill the next day — or the next night, since without Daylight there was no difference between day and night.

Gull agreed to come to the meeting. But it was clear, when he came, that he was not going to change his mind or listen to what Raven said. He had come only because it

35

made him feel even more important to have Raven pleading with him.

'I was made Custodian of Daylight in the beginning of things,' said Gull. 'I am to keep Daylight safe. And I *will* keep it safe.' And he curved his wing tighter round the cedar box.

Raven had run out of words to make Gull see the People's need for light. He thought angrily to himself, 'I wish this Gull would step on a large thorn.'

No sooner had he shaped this thought than Gull cried out, 'Squee! My foot!'

'A thorn, cousin?' asked Raven innocently. 'Let me see — I will take it out for you.'

But of course it was so dark that he could not see the thorn to remove it.

'I must have light to take out the thorn,' said Raven.

'Light? Never!' said Gull.

'Then the thorn will remain.'

Gull complained, and hopped on one foot, and wept, and finally opened his cedar box a crack, so narrow that out glanced a shaft of light no brighter than a single star.

Raven put his hand to Gull's foot, then pretended not to see the thorn. Instead, he pushed it in deeper.

'Squee!' cried Gull. 'My foot!'

'More light, more light!' shouted Raven.

And the lid of the box rose a further crack, so that light gleamed forth like a winter moon. Then Raven reached again for the thorn, and pushed it even further into the soft flesh of Gull's foot.

'More light!' roared Raven.

'Squee, squee, squee!' screamed Gull, and in his pain he flung off the lid of the cedar box.

Like a molten fish the sun slithered from the box, and light and warmth blazed out over the world.

Nor was it ever to be recaptured, no matter how loudly

or how sadly Gull called to it to return to its safe hiding-place beneath his wing.

4

Coyote and Little Blue Fox

SOUTHERN PLAINS

WHEN all the parts of the earth were still glossy with newness, Coyote felt a great enmity for one of the People, Little Blue Fox. It seemed to Coyote that Little Blue Fox was always somehow in his way, upsetting his plans, interfering with his life.

When Coyote went fishing, Little Blue Fox was usually to be found upstream, catching the best fish and leaving none for Coyote. If Coyote were trying to dig a rabbit out of its burrow, Little Blue Fox would lie in wait at the second hole leading out of the burrow, to snap up the rabbit as it escaped. If Coyote wanted a swim in a pool, Little Blue Fox would surely have been there first, stirring up silt and mud into the clear water. If Coyote went to have a meal at a human village, every time Little Blue Fox would be there before him, filling his belly and laughing.

Coyote spent a great deal of time thinking about how often he had been thwarted and disappointed by Little Blue Fox. As he thought about these things he grew angrier and angrier, so that the anger built up like the pressure of water behind a beaver dam. In that state, one day, Coyote saw Little Blue Fox out in open country ahead of him, ambling along, and the dam burst — so that Coyote's anger spilled out in a great shout.

'Little Blue Fox,' Coyote shouted, 'you have caused me enough pain and trouble — you will cause me no more! I am going to tear you to pieces!'

'Oh, please, don't do that, Coyote,' Little Blue Fox said quickly. 'At least not until I have had my fill of prairie chickens.'

'What prairie chickens?' Coyote asked, suddenly both hungry and suspicious at the same time.

41

'Do you see that great tree?' said the Fox, pointing to a mighty pine whose lower branches left marks like those of brooms on the ground. 'A large family of prairie chickens will soon come to meet me there. I have tricked them into believing that I am very ill, and dying, and the mother prairie chicken has promised to bring some medicinal herbs and seeds to cure me. I convinced her that her whole family should come too, so that they could bring me a large supply of seeds. They will be along any minute.'

'Then they will be too late,' Coyote growled, 'for they will find you dead — and not from an illness!' And Coyote gathered himself to spring.

'No, please!' cried Little Blue Fox. 'How can you be so cruel? All my life I have wanted to eat my fill of prairie chicken — just once. And now, when at last my wish is about to come true, you want to kill me. Please, Coyote, let me have my wish, and then kill me — and I will die happily.'

Coyote thought for a moment. 'All right,' he said finally, 'you may have your wish. And then I will have *my* wish — to see you dead.'

'Thank you,' said Fox. 'You are the most generous of the People. And there will probably be enough prairie chicken for you as well.'

'There had better be,' said Coyote, licking his lips.

'Of course,' said Little Blue Fox, 'if they see you here they might turn away. Perhaps you should hide — but somewhere nearby where you can keep an eye on me,' he added hastily.

Coyote nodded. 'A sound idea. Now, I wonder where I could hide?'

'Perhaps you could hide up in the tree itself, and watch me from there,' Little Blue Fox suggested.

'Perhaps I could hide in the tree,' said Coyote as if Little Blue Fox had not spoken, 'and watch you from there.'

'Brilliant!' said Little Blue Fox. 'Why did I not think of that?'

Coyote looked hard at him to see if there was mockery in his expression, but Little Blue Fox's face was still and unsmiling. Never once taking his eyes off the Fox, Coyote turned and began to climb the great tree.

Now, climbing trees was not something that Coyote did well — and large pine trees are unpleasant for any climber. Soon Coyote had to take his eyes off the Fox as he fought to squeeze between tightly tangled branches, or to stretch across spaces where there were no branches. The porcupine-sharp needles of the tree scratched him and seemed unerringly to aim for his eyes. Short twigs on the branches stabbed him; gluey pine gum matted his hair and stuck to his skin; dead branches broke away beneath his feet; scaly bark scrapings fell grittily into his eyes and mouth. It was a slow, arduous and painful climb, but finally — sore, sticky and bleeding — Coyote tucked himself into a high crotch of the tree and peered hopefully down, expecting to see a flock of prairie chickens hurrying to their appointment with Little Blue Fox.

Instead, he saw the Fox himself hurrying off across the plain, kicking up little puffs of dust as he ran.

For a moment Coyote sat perfectly still and quiet in the tree-top. Then he howled — a high, drawn-out howl of pain and rage and humiliation.

Afterwards, he began the slow and tortuous climb down from the tree.

On the ground again, Coyote hurried as fast as his sore feet would allow along the trail left by Little Blue Fox. In spite of his soreness, he was still the fastest runner of the plains — so it was not long before he began to catch sight of the dust trail of Little Blue Fox in the distance every time he topped a rise of land. But Little Blue Fox was looking back, and he too could see the dust-line of Coyote. When Little Blue Fox saw his hunter, he quickly changed direction, seeking the rocky beds of dried streams, or clutches of thorn-bush surrounded by toe-blistering sand.

But Coyote stayed on his trail, though it had become a more painful one to follow.

Shortly Coyote came round a rock outcropping and found himself at a spot where the plain rose suddenly, forming a high, flat-topped hump of land with sheer cliffs along one side of it, slabbed with scales of rock. There, to his astonishment, was Little Blue Fox, standing with his back against the cliff, his legs braced, pushing against the cliff-face with all his strength.

Before Coyote could say anything, Little Blue Fox shouted, 'Thank goodness you have come! Help me quickly — I don't think I can hold it by myself!'

'Hold what?' said the puzzled Coyote. 'What do you think you're doing?'

'The cliff!' shouted the Fox. 'The cliff began to fall and I am holding it back — but I need your help!'

'I'm not listening to any more of your tricks,' Coyote snarled. 'I've listened to you enough. This time I really am going to tear you to bits.'

'Then we will both die,' Little Blue Fox told him, 'for if I let this cliff wall go, it will surely fall on both of us.'

'Lies!' Coyote said. 'That cliff wall has been standing since the beginning of the world and will probably be still standing at the end.'

'No, it is falling!' Little Blue Fox protested, still pushing against the cliff as hard as he could. 'As I came past, some bits of rock trickled down, and I saw that I had to prop up the cliff before all of it collapsed.'

As he spoke, far above them a rabbit became disturbed at the sound of their voices and scrambled into its hole near the edge of the cliff, dislodging a few loose pebbles. They spattered down along the cliff-face and fell directly past Coyote's nose.

'There you are!' cried Little Blue Fox delightedly. 'I am telling you the truth! Now you must help me, for I cannot hold the cliff alone much longer!'

Coyote had given a start of fright as the pebbles fell. Now, convinced, he leaped to the Fox's side and leaned his shoulder as hard as he could against the cliff.

'Push harder!' Little Blue Fox cried. 'Push!' And Coyote strained and heaved against the wall.

'What are we going to do?' Coyote gasped. 'We can't stand here forever holding up this cliff.'

'If only one of us were strong enough to hold it by himself for a while,' said Little Blue Fox, panting with the effort of pushing.

'Why, I'm sure I could hold it,' Coyote said.

'I'm sure you could too,' said Little Blue Fox. 'If you take all the weight, I will go and find a log to prop up the cliff.'

'All right,' said Coyote. He began to push so hard against the cliff that his eyes bulged out and turned red all round their edges. 'Off you go, then,' he grunted. 'But hurry!'

Little Blue Fox pulled away from the wall slowly, as if to make sure that Coyote could really take the strain, stepping back gingerly, then moving away softly as if a heavy footstep might bring the whole cliff crashing down on top of them both.

'Hurry!' Coyote repeated.

'I'll try,' said Little Blue Fox, 'but it may take me a little while to find a log strong enough. Be patient!'

And he rushed off as if his life depended on it – which, of course, it did.

Coyote remained still, his teeth bared and his muscles knotted with strain, forcing his shoulder as hard as he could against the unyielding rock. Soon the shoulder began to feel sore. As time went on, it began to ache fiercely. By then, also, Coyote's head was throbbing from the heat of the sun's direct beams, doubly strong because reflected off the rock wall of the cliff, and his throat was dry and clenched with thirst.

'Where is that Fox?' he muttered to himself. 'Perhaps he

45

is not strong enough to bring a large log quickly. Poor weak thing — it's as well that I came along to hold up this cliff.'

And, proudly, he leaned even harder into the cliff-face and tried to ignore the agony in his shoulder and the fact that his tongue had glued itself to the roof of his mouth with thirst.

But finally, as the day waned and as dusk came to cling to the cliff, he could no longer pretend that he was not suffering.

'I'll have to let the cliff fall, and risk being caught under it,' he said to himself, 'for I will certainly die of thirst if I stay here longer.'

So he gathered up his legs, carefully and slowly, without releasing the pressure against the cliff. Then he made an enormous leap backwards, turning in the air as he went, and ran away from the cliff as fast as only Coyote can run.

Behind him the stillness of the evening remained unbroken. Coyote was not at first aware of the silence. But when he heard no rumble of falling rock, he slowed his pace and looked back over his shoulder.

The cliff had not fallen. It did not look to be in the remotest danger of ever falling, throughout all time.

Coyote could not contain his rage. He howled, he shrieked, he leaped into the air, he rolled on the ground, he ran around in small circles snapping at shadows.

'Now he has gone too far!' Coyote screamed. 'Too far! I will tear out his tongue! I will pull off his head! I will. . .' Unable to think of any more terrible things to do to Little Blue Fox, he raced off through the evening in the direction the Fox had taken.

Soon Coyote's nose told him he was approaching a small lake, which reminded him all over again how painfully thirsty he had been, before his anger turned his mind away from it.

'Little Blue Fox is thirsty too,' Coyote muttered to himself. 'Now I will catch him.'

Through a small stand of trees Coyote rushed down to bury his face in the lake's cool surface. But there he slid to a hasty stop, unable to believe his eyes.

As if nothing had happened, Little Blue Fox was standing quietly by the side of the lake, outlined by the light of the moon that had just climbed above the nearby trees.

'Drink before you do anything else,' Little Blue Fox said gently. 'It will make you feel much better.'

'I will not!' shouted the raging Coyote. 'I will never again do anything you say! I am going to tear you to pieces this minute, without delay!'

'Don't be foolish,' Little Blue Fox said, stepping nearer to Coyote. 'You ought to have a drink before killing me, so you can enjoy it more. Here — if you hold on to my arm you will know I cannot get away, so you may drink in peace. The water is cool from fresh underground streams.'

By then, all the talk of drinking had made Coyote's thirst even more desperate. Without a word, he roughly grasped Fox's wrist and turned to plunge his face into the water, gulping until he had to stop for breath.

'I'm glad you came along,' Little Blue Fox said genially. 'I was hoping some strong swimmer would come to help me retrieve that large maize cake out there in the water.'

Coyote raised his dripping face and looked at the lake. As the ripples from his drinking smoothed, he saw what seemed to be a large yellow disc lying in the darkened water.

'I went to a great deal of trouble to get that cake from the humans,' Fox went on. 'Now if someone doesn't hurry and dive for it, it will sink beyond reach. Just look at the size of it.'

Coyote looked, and his stomach turned over with hunger.

'How did the cake come to be in the lake?' Coyote asked with suspicion.

'I was on my way back to you,' Little Blue Fox said airily, 'when I stopped here for a drink and stupidly let the cake drop into the water.'

47

Coyote paused, unable to think clearly for the noise his stomach was making. 'I don't think even I can dive that deeply.'

'There is a way,' Fox said thoughtfully. 'You could tie a large stone round your neck, which would make you heavy enough to sink down to the cake.'

'Perhaps I could tie a large stone round my neck,' Coyote said, again as if Little Blue Fox had not spoken, 'and let it sink me down to the cake.'

'Wonderful!' said Little Blue Fox. 'How clever you are.'

'I can already taste the delicious flavour of maize cake,' said Coyote gleefully.

He bounded off and found the biggest rock he could carry, while Fox swiftly twisted together some grass fibres to make a short and sturdy rope. Then he tied the rope to the rock. Coyote helpfully lifted his chin while Fox tied the other end round his neck. Then they went to the edge of the lake, where a ledge of mossy rock jutted out above the deepest part.

'Now,' said Little Blue Fox, 'I will throw the rock as far as I can from this edge and at the same time you jump.'

Coyote peered over the edge at the still surface of the lake. 'Are you quite sure. . .?' he began.

But Fox cut in quickly. 'Remember the delicious taste of maize cake,' he said. 'All you need to do is jump, and soon your belly will be full.'

As if it had heard, Coyote's stomach gave a loud rumble. 'All right,' said Coyote, 'here I go.'

Little Blue Fox picked up the rock and, with a mighty heave, threw it over the edge of the outcropping, and Coyote leaped out and plunged down into the water.

Chuckling to himself, Fox watched for a moment as the rock dragged Coyote down into the black depths, with Coyote looking this way and that for the maize cake. But it was not to be found, for of course the yellow disc had been the reflection of the full moon, which Coyote had been too hungry and too impatient to notice. Then, still laughing, Little Blue Fox ran off into the darkness.

What seemed a very long time later, Coyote came to the surface of the lake and scrabbled weakly out of the water. There on the lake's edge he lay still — exhausted, half-starved, half-drowned. By the time he was able to stand up, Little Blue Fox was far, far away.

'I think I will leave that Fox alone from now on,' Coyote thought to himself as he stumbled back to his home, 'for he will surely kill me dead if we meet again.'

5

Coyote and the Mice

CENTRAL PLAINS

ONE day during a summer in the world's beginning when rain came only in the early season of the sun, Coyote was travelling across the prairie. The heat dried his tongue and lips until it seemed that they would crack like the hard-baked surface of the soil. So he felt great relief when dusk brought the coolness of a prairie evening, and when he came to a small creek with a trickle of water still in it. There he found a copse of birch, white poplar and willow trees, and there too was a shallow grassy dip in the ground, just big enough for his body, and still cupping within itself some of the warmth of the day.

So Coyote curled round and lay down in that welcome bed, exhausted and ready for a long sleep. But the night was full of disturbance. He spent much of it sneezing mosquitoes away from his nose and listening to them whine spitefully around his ears. And he sneezed even more when a chill eastern breeze arose to wipe away the last of the warmth from the ground. But at last he drifted into a rest-less, fretful sleep, and managed even to stay in it while shivering under the silver-cold full moon that rose later to glare down on to his bed.

But then the moonlight brought out the worst distur-bance of all. A horde of mice — Coyote felt there were hundreds — came running down to the creek, and skittered over Coyote's legs and body as if he were no more than a log lying in their path.

Angrily, but not fully awake, Coyote threshed about under their tiny scratching paws and flailed with his legs. 'Can you not find another path?' he growled, then rolled over to resume his sleep.

For a long few moments there was stillness and silence

around him, as if the mice had mysteriously vanished. Then through his hazy, weary half-sleep Coyote heard all the mouse voices raised in a high, shrill crying — louder than the whine of mosquitoes, but just as maddening.

'Be quiet!' Coyote grumbled from his sleep. 'Go and do your singing somewhere else!' And he kicked out again with his legs into the grass around him, and rolled over again hoping to find a more comfortable position that would take him down into the deeper sleep he craved.

But instead he was brought fully awake, for the high-pitched keening rose even more loudly, until it seemed to scrape at his very eardrums.

'Stop that noise!' shouted Coyote, and rose to his feet in rage.

At once he saw the reason for the shrill crying sound. All around him in the grassy hollow where he had made his bed lay the tiny bodies of dead mice — killed by the threshing and rolling and kicking that he had done, trying to preserve his restless sleep. And the high keening was the noise of grief, being made by the many dozens of living mice weeping among their dead.

Coyote felt a small bitter tendril of guilt creep within his belly, at the sight of the slaughter and pain he had caused. But guilt is an uncomfortable feeling, and Coyote quickly hid it from himself. He hid it by covering it up, with anger and with blame.

'Be off!' he shouted. 'None of this would have happened had you not come along to interrupt my sleep! Now get away, and disturb me no more!'

And he lunged towards the mice, with a snarl and a flash of teeth, till they scrambled away for safety.

In the quiet that the mice left behind them, Coyote once again curled himself into the shallow hole — well away from the tiny still bodies — and closed his eyes, gritty with lack of sleep.

Full daylight and the risen sun were penetrating the

leaves of the copse by the time he awakened. And once again he was brought out of his sleep by the shrill cries of mice. But this time the cries filled Coyote with fear, not anger. They were the sort of cries made by creatures of the wilderness when they sense the coming of a great terror — fire or flood or windstorm.

Coyote leaped up, hardly noticing that some time in the night the dead mice had been silently removed from the hollow. 'What is it?' he cried. 'What is happening?'

'Run, Coyote! Hide!' shouted the mice, rushing towards him. 'A mighty hailstorm is sweeping across the land, with ice-stones the size of your head falling to crush any living thing beneath them! We must all hide!'

'But you have only to creep into your holes and burrows to be safe,' cried Coyote, almost weeping with fear. 'What shall I do? Where can I hide?'

'We are not as safe as you think,' said one of the older mice. 'We cannot all get into our burrows at once — there are too many of us. We are never all together in our nests at the same time, because some of us are guarding the entrances, and many others are out gathering food. So most of us here will have to stay above ground during the storm.'

'But how will you protect yourselves? How will I protect myself?' whimpered Coyote.

'We have a way,' said another mouse. 'We climb into bags of especially tough buffalo hide, then with ropes we pull ourselves up into the trees where the boughs and leaves are extra protection.'

'What a clever idea,' said Coyote. 'I hope you have a hide-bag big enough for me?'

'But why should we help you,' said several mice, 'when you cruelly and carelessly killed so many of us during the night, without showing any sympathy?'

With those words, that small tendril of guilt inside Coyote grew suddenly larger, strengthened by his fear.

55

Tears sprang from his eyes as he fell on his knees before the mice, babbling apologies, begging forgiveness, praying that they would help him now in spite of what had happened the night before.

'You would not let the storm kill me,' he wept, 'because of something I did while I was half asleep and not paying proper attention?'

At that, a grandmotherly mouse stepped forward. 'We could say that you *should* have been paying attention, to the lives of other creatures. But let that now all be past. Here is a bag that will hold you. Into it quickly, now, for the sky is darkening.'

So it was, as Coyote saw with a fearful glance upwards. Of course, it was the time of year, as he knew, when the north wind often blew heavy low clouds over the plain. But Coyote did not stop to think too long about clouds. He watched the mice scrambling into their bags, and the darting swiftness of their movements infected him with a new panic. Hastily he climbed into his own bag, first throwing the rope from the bag's drawstring up over a tree branch, as he had seen the mice do. Then, his arms extended out of the neck of the bag, he pulled himself up until he was swinging in mid-air. Finally he knotted the other end of the rope on to the drawstring and pulled his arms into the bag, while his own weight drew the neck of the bag tightly closed.

Then he waited, inside the stifling bag. The rough and dusty hair of the hide had been turned inwards, and as he tried to find a comfortable position his nose became irritated and his eyes began to run. Worse still, his movements caused the bag to swing, and the springiness of the branch it was tied to kept up a steady rocking, lurching motion so that Coyote began to feel decidedly sick.

But he curled up in a tight ball, telling himself that any discomfort and hardship was better than being killed by a downpour of enormous hailstones. And just as that thought crossed his mind, a gust of wind swung the bag even more strongly, and he heard the shrieking of the mice.

'Here comes the hail! Here comes the hail!'

And as he heard it, he felt a sharp impact and a blazing pain on his side — and another blow almost at the same time on a knee — and another agonizing blow on his lower back — and more blows, and bruising pains, all over his back and bottom and legs and shoulders and head, any place that was touching the hide — and more, and more. . . .

Some little distance from the copse of trees where Coyote was in such pain, a group of the People walked quietly together, talking of many things. Some had looked up to notice that the wind was clearing away the low, churning bank of black clouds that had blown up — and that wide stretches of blue sky were beginning to appear. As they walked, the People suddenly became aware of a loud shrieking and howling that was coming from a small stand of trees nearby.

They hurried over to find out the cause of the noise. When they reached the copse, they stood silent with amazement.

They saw a large, bulging bag of buffalo hide suspended from the branch of a tree. And beneath it they saw dozens upon dozens of mice, pelting the bag with a barrage of sharp stones which other mice were carrying up from the nearby creek-bed.

'Ow, ow, owooooooo!' howled the bag, in the unmistakable voice of Coyote.

'Oh, ow, the pain, help, oh!' shouted the mice, not pausing in their hurling of stones. 'The hail is getting worse, the hailstones are getting bigger!'

'They are, they are!' wailed Coyote. 'Ow, owooo!'

And so they were, for the mice were now gathering and flinging the largest stones they could find, and so many of them that they rattled against the hide-bag and its bruised contents with the speed of real hail.

At this point Quail, who had a tender heart and could not bear any form of cruelty, stepped from the watching group of the People.

'Why are you doing this?' she asked one of the mice, who was gathering stones nearby. 'You will kill him.'

In reply the mouse led Quail deeper into the copse of trees, and pointed out the bodies of her two children, lying among the other mice that had died the night before.

'They died because Coyote was careless and indifferent to others,' said the mouse. 'We do not intend to kill him — only to teach him a lesson about suffering, about paying attention to other creatures. There would be no point in killing him, for then there would be no learning.'

In a short while the cries and howls from the hide-bag began to grow weaker, and at a sign from one of their elders the mice put down their last stones and lowered the bag out of the tree. They pulled the drawstring open, and there lay Coyote — unable to move, dreadfully battered, covered with lumps and bruises. At first he could not even see, for swellings around his eyes had squeezed them shut. But the mice bathed his head and face in sweet balsam water, and finally he managed to raise an eyelid and look around him.

He saw the People, standing beyond the mice, watching as quietly as the shadows of the trees behind them. He saw the mice, also standing silently, looking altogether healthy and unaffected by any hailstorm. He saw the sky, clear blue now, entirely free of clouds. He saw the dry, dry ground.

But, most vividly, he saw the huge pile of stones, large and small, strewn beneath and around the tree where he had hung as helpless as a bird's nest.

Coyote stared foolishly at all these sights. He could see exactly what had happened. And, deep within himself, where that tendril of guilt coiled and grew, he knew exactly why it had happened.

Slowly, dazedly, with every sore place on his body crying out in pain, he struggled to his feet.

'Why,' he said, 'you have tricked me half to death.'

6

Raven's Companion

PACIFIC NORTH WEST

In those long-ago days when the making of the world had been fully finished, all the seas and forests and mountains, all the stones and plants and living creatures and human beings, the days seemed slow and heavy to Raven, time moved like a winter river. He could always find some sort of thing to do: explore wide streams where salmon plunged in springtime; seek high ledges above tree-reflecting lakes for peaceful thinking and remembering; pay a visit to another of the People, Bear or Eagle or Fox. But though these were enjoyable things to do, when he returned to his home — in a cave carved by winds in a mountain's uppermost crag — the days still seemed to have been empty.

Finally this heavy, dissatisfied feeling grew so strong that Raven could no longer bear it. He went to seek the advice of Mountain Sheep, who made his home on a pinnacle almost as high as Raven's. There Raven found him, his fleece gleaming as thick and white as the clouds that the mountains wore like a collar, some distance below their peaks.

'So you are restless?' asked Mountain Sheep when Raven had explained his trouble. 'Without interest in life? Each moment does not deal with itself before the next moment is upon you?'

'Yes, all of that,' said Raven.

Mountain Sheep stared thoughtfully out over the peaks, and remained motionless for so long that Raven began to think he had gone to sleep. So Raven shuffled his feet a little and made a small croaking cough in the back of his throat.

Mountain Sheep looked at him, blinked, then snorted and tossed his head up and down two or three times to show that he had been awake all the time.

'It is all very clear,' he said, and tossed his head again as if to make it clearer.

'Is it?' said Raven, puzzled.

'It seems to me you're lonely,' said Mountain Sheep.

Now it was Raven's turn to stare out over the mountains and ponder. He had always been alone — but then for so long the days had been full and busy while he was playing his part in the laborious making of the earth. Now, with so much more time to use up, perhaps it was indeed loneliness that was making him feel so strange.

'You need a companion,' Mountain Sheep went on. 'Someone to be with you always, to share your days and to talk with at night about the day's events.'

'You're right,' said Raven. 'But where can I find such a companion?'

'I can't help you with that,' said Mountain Sheep.

So Raven thanked him, and then returned home and thought. None of the People would come and live with him always, that was certain. Nor would any human being, since they preferred their own kind. And other living creatures would not be such enjoyable companions, because their thinking powers and their conversation did not offer as much as Raven would want.

'Is there no companion on the earth for Raven?' he asked the wind.

The wind went about its business and made no reply, but almost in the asking of the question Raven had his answer.

'I have made other creatures and brought them alive on the earth,' he said to himself. 'I will make one now to be my companion.'

The next day Raven flew to a lake deep within the nearby forests where, at the edge of the cold blue water, there could be found especially fine white clay. Taking a scoop of the clay back to his high cave, he carefully fashioned a large egg, moulding its surface to such smoothness that it seemed exactly as if a giant bird had laid it.

Then he began the labours that would bring the egg to life. First he built an enormous fire, placing on it thoroughly seasoned cedar wood, handfuls of special roots, and bunches of aromatic herbs which he gathered from the forest. As these materials burned, Raven busily scraped up their ashes and placed them in a smooth granite mortar where with a pestle he ground them into a fine dust. Though every stray breeze would lift this dust into the air, Raven was able to pour it into large wooden bowls, and then he dropped in red-hot pebbles from the fireside to warm the dust. When it had warmed through, Raven poured the dust out of the bowls around the egg.

He repeated the process over and over, each time brushing away the cooled ash from the egg. At the same time, while grinding and heating and pouring, Raven had also to keep the fire fed with the proper wood and roots and herbs, which meant many hasty trips to the forest. He worked so hard and so quickly that the egg stayed warm in its bed of fine ash for seven times seven days, and at the end of that time Raven's labours came to an end.

At sunrise on the fiftieth day, the egg moved and rocked, and Raven sat back to watch. He was too exhausted to do more, even if there had been more to do. He had not slept for the whole time of the ritual, his muscles ached from the continual grinding with the heavy pestle, and his eyes were painfully swollen from lack of sleep and the irritation of the fire's smoke and the drifting of the fine ash. In fact he had his stinging eyes closed, to ease them, at the very instant that the egg cracked open.

When Raven first opened his eyes all he could see was an immense cloud of dust, with a flurry of feathered wings somewhere at its centre. Raven began to cough, and the flurry stopped. Slowly the dark ash began to settle on the creature who had stirred it up, and whom Raven could still not clearly see.

'Hello,' the creature suddenly said, 'I'm here. Who are you?'

'I'm Raven,' said Raven. 'I made you.'

'Good,' said the creature cheerfully. 'Am I a Raven too?'

For a moment Raven was unable to think of a reply, for the dust had finally settled, revealing the whole of the being he had made. It was a kind of bird, but there was no other bird like it in the world. Every feather was a different size and shape from every other, and every one glinted with a different colour as well — all the reds and browns and yellows and greens and blues imaginable, and more besides.

Its beak was curled and twisted like the tendrils of the climbing vine. One foot was flat and webbed, the other was taloned like the hawk's. One wing was that of a hummingbird, the other was the wing of a heron. On its chest was a vast plume of feathers, so thick and long that the creature could lean forward against it for extra support, as if from a third leg. And its tail — Raven could only shake his head in amazement — was made of long, coarse hair that curled at the tips.

'No,' said Raven at last, 'you are not a Raven. You are something altogether special.'

'Good,' said the bird again. 'Why did you make me?'

'Because I was alone,' said Raven. 'You are to be my friend and companion.'

'All right,' said the bird. 'What do friends and companions do?'

'You will fly with me,' said Raven, 'and share my adventures, and talk about them with me in the quiet hours of evening, and share all my thoughts and feelings.'

'All right,' said the bird as brightly as before. 'How do you fly?'

'Come outside and I will teach you,' said Raven.

The strange bird willingly started for the door of the cave. But with his first steps the clawed foot dug too deeply into the earth floor, while the webbed foot slipped on a heap of fine ash. Suddenly the creature was toppling forward, squawking, his wings threshing. The plume of feathers on his chest spread out and broke his fall, but managed only to turn him sideways and then entirely over, so that he fell on to his back. There he lay, his wings flailing up another huge cloud of ash, his feet waving feebly in the air.

Raven might have laughed if he had not been coughing again. Seeing that his companion would never be a very skilled walker, Raven pushed him outside to the broad ledge that lay before the cave, and there helped him to his feet and dusted off his wildly coloured feathers.

'Now are you ready to fly?' he asked.

'Yes,' said the bird, looking determined.

'Then watch,' said Raven.

And he leaned slightly forward into the mountain-top wind, spread his wings, and rose lightly into the air, soaring and wheeling above the upturned head of the strange bird. 'Come and join me,' he called.

'How?' asked the bird.

'Just take a deep breath, lean into the wind, and scoop up the air with the lower part of your wings.'

So the bird leaned forward, his eyes clamped shut, his plume of feathers spread wide and trembling, and began flapping his wings. The hummingbird wing moved so quickly that Raven could hardly see it, but the great heron wing thrust at the air only twice before the bird lifted awkwardly into the air, rising above the ledge up to where Raven circled.

The bird's eyes — which Raven now noticed were different colours, one yellow and one blue — snapped wide open with astonishment. Then he looked down.

'Help!' he squawked. 'I will fall and break into pieces!'

'No, you won't,' called Raven. 'Just keep moving your wings, and you will fly.'

67

'No — I will fall!' cried the terrified bird. And so, of course, he did — headfirst on to the ledge, where his curly beak stuck fast like the point of an arrow.

Raven descended and pulled the bird free by his hairy tail. 'That was fine,' he said, 'for the first time. When you fly again, remember to keep your wings moving.'

'I don't want to fly any more,' moaned the bird. 'It frightens me.'

'But you must fly,' said Raven. 'You are a bird, and birds fly.'

The bird looked down at his feet, then nervously up at the sky. 'All right,' he said.

'Now I'll teach you some other things about flying,' said Raven. 'Besides keeping your wings moving, you must remember that if you want to turn to the right, you lower your right wing and raise your left wing. If you want to turn to the left, you lower your left wing and raise your right wing.'

The bird blinked a few times, then stared at his wings. 'Which is my right wing, and which is my left?'

'Your right wing is on the right side of your body,' said Raven, 'and your left wing is on your left side.'

'But which is my right side and which is my left?'

Raven sighed. 'That is your right wing,' he said, pointing to the heron wing, 'and that is your left,' pointing to the hummingbird wing. 'Now we will try again.'

Together they leaned into the wind, flapped their wings and rose lightly from the ledge. Side by side they flew upwards, and as they flew Raven felt the joy of companionship, the deep pleasure of a shared moment. He gazed fondly at the bird he had made. Surely this would be a fine, close companion, for all its strange and garish appearance.

'You're doing well,' Raven called. 'Now turn left!'

As he spoke, Raven lowered his left wing and began a graceful arc around to his left. But before he could change direction or even call out, the other bird dipped his right wing, the heron wing, and swerved sharply around to the right.

They collided head-on, entangling wings and feet, and fell in a screeching, fluttering mass to the hard ledge below.

This time the newly made bird fell on to its cushioning chest plume, and Raven landed on his companion's back. So neither was badly hurt, though Raven got up from the tangle rubbing several painfully bruised places on his body.

'Never mind,' he said. 'You will learn to tell left from right soon enough. In the meantime I must teach you another important thing about flying.'

At this the strange bird looked so terrified that Raven hurried on to say, 'This next thing is easier than telling left from right. I promise you will not fall again. Besides, you fly into the air very well; now you must learn what to do when you are up there.'

'All right,' said the bird, no longer sounding cheerful nor looking determined.

'This lesson has to do with flying high and with landing,' said Raven. 'When you want to come down to land, you must lower your tail and raise your wings, so that you will float back down to earth feet first.'

'That doesn't sound difficult,' said the other bird dubiously.

'Should you want to fly even higher, though,' Raven went on, 'your tail stays up and your wings thrust down.'

'I understand,' said the bird. 'To fly down, tail down. To fly up, tail up.'

'Exactly!' said Raven enthusiastically. 'Now we can try it.'

Once again they moved their wings together – or as much together as heron and hummingbird and raven wings could be – and rose into the air. Then Raven called, 'Now let us go down again!'

But as· Raven began to descend, he discovered that his new companion did not know up from down any better than he had known left from right. As powerfully as he could, the strange bird beat his mis-matched wings downwards, and thrust his hairy tail as far upwards as it would go. Naturally, he shot up at great speed higher and higher into the air.

The startled Raven stared for a moment, then launched himself upwards in pursuit. 'Come back, come back!' he called. 'Tail down, wings up!'

But the other bird was much too high to hear him and, with his wings beating mightily, was rising far too quickly for Raven to catch up. So Raven circled sadly and watched his strange creation rise farther and farther up into the blue, until he seemed to shrink in size to that of a speck of dust, then finally to disappear altogether.

Raven went quietly back to his cave and cleared up the mess he had made, deciding that it was not so terrible after all to live alone. And to this day the peculiar bird he had made has never been seen again, by Raven or by anyone else.

7

Coyote and the Giant Lizard

CHINOOK

WHEN the animals of the world were first made, there were many among them which no longer live today, but sometimes haunt our dreams. One such was a giant lizard, which roamed the land and terrorized all living creatures. It was as long as the tallest tree was high, its teeth were as large and sharp as the biggest hunting knives, and each of its footprints was the size of the hugest boulder in the mountains. Its passing shook the trees and made the ground throb like the hide on a war-drum. And the sound of its roar echoed through all the swampy valleys, rising far up to the forested hill-tops.

The giant lizard was an eater of meat. And it favoured above all the meat of human beings, who could not run as fast nor fight as fiercely as other creatures. So it constantly raided the camps of men, and always did so at night. It would charge out of the darkness into a sleeping village, bellowing with hunger and the killing urge, red eyes gleaming like flames in a bake-pit. Its claws would slit open the lodges as a fisherman opens his fish, and women and children would spill out, screaming, running to find hiding-places in the rocks or bushes.

The warriors would stand bravely against the monster, but their arrows and spears were as useless against its flinty hide as pine needles against an avalanche. The terrible head would swing down, the cavernous jaws would gape, and some of the warriors would die. Then, beyond the camp, in the blackness where the lizard could see as well as a hawk sees by day, it would hunt the women and children who had not found safe hiding-places, until it had eaten its fill.

One day Coyote happened to come through the hills to

a village that had been destroyed by the monster on the previous night. He looked with wonder at the weeping men and women picking up their scattered belongings, trying to rebuild their lodges, or searching and calling through the nearby bush in the hope that some of their loved ones who were still missing might after all have saved themselves.

Coyote asked the chief what great mischief had happened, and the man told him about the night terror of his people.

'Why does the great lizard come only at night?' asked Coyote.

'I have heard that it is almost blind in the light of day,' said the chief. 'It must return to its dark cave with the first gleam of morning that scatters the mists upon the mountain peaks.'

'And where is its cave?' asked Coyote.

The chief shrugged. 'I have heard only that it is the deepest cave in the largest valley. I do not know where that is to be found.'

'Never mind,' said Coyote. 'I will find it. And when I do, your people will no longer have reason to fear the coming of this creature.'

So Coyote went into the mountains, running along the ridges among the high peaks, until he came at last to an immense valley, so long that it would take the strongest man two days to run the length of it. There Coyote saw the mouth of a great cave, and he knew by the foul smell around it that it was the cave of the giant lizard.

Coyote waited until that time of day when the sun is at its brightest, and shadows are at their shortest. Then he took his bow and arrows and climbed to the topmost peak of the highest mountain. Fitting an arrow to his bow, he aimed and shot it into the sun. Then he shot another arrow into the butt-end of the first arrow's shaft. Then he shot another into the butt of the second arrow. Arrow after arrow followed, shot into one another to form a long arrow-chain that reached from the sun to the mountain-top

74

where Coyote stood.

He grasped this chain and pulled, to drag the sun free from the sky. He tugged and jerked, and the sky wrinkled and bulged, and just as he began to fear that the entire sky would be torn away, the sun came loose and Coyote dragged it down on to the mountain-top. Quickly he pulled it to a river and pinned it with his arrows beneath the water.

Darkness fell upon the land. From within the depths of its lair, the giant lizard saw the light wink out from the mouth of its cave, and it lumbered forth, filling the valley with the voice of its hunger. The thunder of its roaring echoed into distant valleys, where warriors reached for their spears, wondering at the sun's short day, fearing an unnatural length to the night. And women and children fled to find rock crevices or other spots safe from the mighty teeth and claws.

When the lizard had gone the distance from its cave that a strong man could run in one day, Coyote pulled out the arrows that held the sun beneath the river. Like a released willow-branch snare, the sun sprang back at once to its place in the sky. Its glare spread over the world, welcome to the hiding humans but striking like spears at the eyes of the monster.

The lizard roared with fright, and turned to make its way blindly back to the cave. Then Coyote sprang down from the mountain and stood before it. With the haft of his bow he struck the lizard a mighty blow on the tenderest part of its nose. The lizard screamed its pain and wrath, and reared up, casting its shadow half the length of the valley. Coyote sprang away as its long neck whipped the fearsome head around in great arcs while the longer tail splintered trees with its lashing.

'Over here!' shouted Coyote. 'It is I, Coyote, who struck you! I am here!'

The lizard, whose brain was as small as a peewit's eye in spite of the vastness of its body, rushed towards the sound

of Coyote's voice. Taunting and laughing, Coyote turned
and ran, keeping just out of reach of the blind monster's
slashing jaws. Soon the lizard tired, and the pace of its
charge began to slow. Then Coyote leaped and swung his
bow again, striking the same spot on its nose, and shouting,
'Here I am! Come and catch me!'

Once more the lizard filled the valleys with its bellowing,
and charged towards the mocking voice, but with no more
chance of overtaking the fleet Coyote than of catching a
swallow's wing. Again and again, when the monster seemed
to be tiring of the chase, Coyote would strike it on the nose
and make it rush after him, farther into the valley.

In this way Coyote led the blind and furious lizard to
the edge of the deepest swamp in the land. There Coyote
leaped lightly and easily across hillocks of grass to firm
ground on the other side of the swamp. But the lizard, still
blindly pursuing him, blundered with its enormous weight
into the heart of the swamp. With all its giant strength it
fought to keep going, but the black lake of mud slowed it
and stopped it, sucked it down and swallowed it up
entirely.

And so the human beings were free at last to sleep
unafraid in the peace of their lodges.

8

How Coyote Stole Fire

CROW

LONG ago, when man was newly come into the world, there were days when he was the happiest creature of all. Those were the days when spring brushed across the willow tails, or when his children ripened with the blueberries in the sun of summer, or when the goldenrod bloomed in the autumn haze.

But always the mists of autumn evenings grew more chill, and the sun's strokes grew shorter. Then man saw winter moving near, and he became fearful and unhappy. He was afraid for his children, and for the grandfathers and grandmothers who carried in their heads the sacred tales of the tribe. Many of these, young and old, would die in the long, ice-bitter months of winter.

Coyote, like the rest of the People, had no need for fire. So he seldom concerned himself with it, until one spring day when he was passing a human village. There the women were singing a song of mourning for the babies and the old ones who had died in the winter. Their voices moaned like the west wind through a buffalo skull, prickling the hairs on Coyote's neck.

'Feel how the sun is now warm on our backs,' one of the men was saying. 'Feel how it warms the earth and makes these stones hot to the touch. If only we could have had a small piece of the sun in our teepees during the winter.'

Coyote, overhearing this, felt sorry for the men and women. He also felt that there was something he could do to help them. He knew of a faraway mountain-top where the three Fire Beings lived. These Beings kept fire to themselves, guarding it carefully for fear that man might somehow acquire it and become as strong as they. Coyote saw that he could do a good turn for man at the expense of these selfish Fire Beings.

So Coyote went to the mountain of the Fire Beings and crept to its top, to watch the way that the Beings guarded their fire. As he came near, the Beings leaped to their feet and gazed searchingly round their camp. Their eyes glinted like bloodstones, and their hands were clawed like the talons of the great black vulture.

'What's that? What's that I hear?' hissed one of the Beings.

'A thief, skulking in the bushes!' screeched another.

The third looked more closely, and saw Coyote. But he had gone to the mountain-top on all-fours, so the Being thought she saw only an ordinary coyote slinking among the trees.

'It is no one, it is nothing!' she cried, and the other two looked where she pointed and also saw only a grey coyote. They sat down again by their fire and paid Coyote no more attention.

So he watched all day and night as the Fire Beings guarded their fire. He saw how they fed it pine cones and dry branches from the sycamore trees. He saw how they stamped furiously on runaway rivulets of flame that sometimes nibbled outwards on edges of dry grass. He saw also how, at night, the Beings took turns to sit by the fire. Two would sleep while one was on guard; and at certain times the Being by the fire would get up and go into their teepee, and another would come out to sit by the fire.

Coyote saw that the Beings were always jealously watchful of their fire except during one part of the day. That was in the earliest morning, when the first winds of dawn arose on the mountains. Then the Being by the fire would hurry, shivering, into the teepee calling, 'Sister, sister, go out and watch the fire.' But the next Being would always be slow to go out for her turn, her head spinning with sleep and the thin dreams of dawn.

Coyote, seeing all this, went down the mountain and

spoke to some of his friends among the People. He told them of hairless man, fearing the cold and death of winter. And he told them of the Fire Beings, and the warmth and brightness of the flame. They all agreed that man should have fire, and they all promised to help Coyote's undertaking.

Then Coyote sped again to the mountain-top. Again the Fire Beings leaped up when he came close, and one cried out, 'What's that? A thief, a thief!'

But again the others looked closely, and saw only a grey coyote hunting among the bushes. So they sat down again and paid him no more attention.

Coyote waited through the day, and watched as night fell and two of the Beings went off to the teepee to sleep. He watched as they changed over at certain times all the night long, until at last the dawn winds rose.

Then the Being on guard called, 'Sister, sister, get up and watch the fire.'

And the Being whose turn it was climbed slow and sleepy from her bed, saying, 'Yes, yes, I am coming. Do not shout so.'

But before she could come out of the teepee, Coyote lunged from the bushes, snatched up a glowing portion of fire, and sprang away down the mountainside.

Screaming, the Fire Beings flew after him. Swift as Coyote ran, they caught up with him, and one of them reached out a clutching hand. Her fingers touched only the tip of the tail, but the touch was enough to turn the hairs white, and coyote tail-tips are white still. Coyote shouted, and flung the fire away from him. But the others of the People had gathered at the mountain's foot, in case they were needed. Squirrel saw the fire falling, and caught it, putting it on her back and fleeing away through the tree-tops. The fire scorched her back so painfully that her tail curled up and back, as squirrels' tails still do today.

The Fire Beings then pursued Squirrel, who threw the fire to Chipmunk. Chattering with fear, Chipmunk stood

81

still as if rooted until the Beings were almost upon her. Then, as she turned to run, one Being clawed at her, tearing down the length of her back and leaving three stripes that are to be seen on chipmunks' backs even today. Chipmunk threw the fire to Frog, and the Beings turned towards him. One of the Beings grasped his tail, but Frog gave a mighty leap and tore himself free, leaving his tail behind in the Being's hand — which is why frogs have had no tails ever since.

As the Beings came after him again, Frog flung the fire on to Wood. And Wood swallowed it.

The Fire Beings gathered round, but they did not know how to get the fire out of Wood. They promised it gifts, sang to it and shouted at it. They twisted it and struck it and tore it with their knives. But Wood did not give up the fire. In the end, defeated, the Beings went back to their mountain-top and left the People alone.

But Coyote knew how to get fire out of Wood. And he went to the village of men and showed them how. He showed them the trick of rubbing two dry sticks together, and the trick of spinning a sharpened stick in a hole made in another piece of wood. So man was from then on warm and safe through the killing cold of winter.

9

Raven and the Whale

ESKIMO

Once, long before the ocean shores had been rubbed smooth by waves, Raven was fishing by plunging into the sea, and soon had gathered a great heap of fish of every kind. He then came back to shore and took up the sticks that he carried with him to make fire, planning to cook and eat all of the fish he had caught — for as everyone knows Raven is the greediest of the People.

When he had a large fire of driftwood blazing up, he became busy spearing the fish one at a time on a green willow sapling, roasting them over the flames and gobbling them only half-cooked. But then, when the worst of his hunger-ache had eased, he began thinking about how he gathered his food and cooked it.

'There must be a less tiring way for me to fill my belly properly,' he thought. 'Having to catch each of these little fish, then having to roast each of them in turn, is hard work. I never seem to get enough at once to feel satisfied.'

He tried spitting two or three fish at the same time on the willow stick, but even that did not seem enough. Pondering the problem, he gazed out to sea, where the sun was turning the blue wave-tops to silver and gold. And there, as he gazed, came the answer he wanted.

It came in the form of bursts of water erupting skyward from the heart of a wave, followed by a number of broad, bulky shadows shouldering their way to the sea's surface.

'Whales!' Raven said aloud. 'That's what I need. If I could catch a whale and cook it, I would have enough food to satisfy me!'

So, gathering up his belongings, he rose in the air and flew out towards the herd of whales. As he came closer to the whales he flew lower, until he was nearly skimming the wave ridges. And that was a dangerous mistake. Suddenly, beneath him, the water exploded in a thrashing foam, and an enormous whale leaped, her vast mouth gaping. Then her mouth closed over Raven, and he fell through echoing darkness while the whale's huge body splashed back into the sea.

Raven struck something warmly moist and soft that stopped his fall painlessly, then sat up and looked around. He found that he was inside a vast, open area like a cavern, surrounded by the smooth, rubbery flesh of the whale, with its spine and its great ribs arching far above him. All around him he could hear the rhythmic beat of a mighty heart, like distant thunder echoing in Raven's mountain home. He could see quite well because at the far end of the cave there was, astonishingly, a softly glowing lamp. As he moved towards it for a closer look, out of the shadows — even more surprisingly — stepped a beautiful girl.

'How did you come here?' asked the girl. Her voice was soft and her smile gentle. 'You are the first person to enter this place.'

'The whale ate me,' said Raven simply. 'How did you come here? Have you been swallowed too?'

The girl laughed. 'No, I have been here as long as the whale has lived. I am the spirit of the whale.'

'If you are the whale's spirit,' Raven said, 'then you can tell me how I can get out again.'

'I cannot help you,' the girl said. 'I would not know anything about how to leave the whale. But do you have to leave right away? Could you not stay with me a while?'

'I could,' Raven said. 'But I must warn you that I become very hungry, very easily, and there does not seem to be much to eat in here.'

'Oh, but there is,' said the girl. 'I can go and gather fish that the whale has swallowed. Shall I get some for you now?'

'That would be very kind,' said Raven, even though not

long before he had eaten a great many fish.

'Very well. But while I am gone,' the girl said, 'you must not for any reason touch my lamp.'

Raven looked more closely at the lamp. He could see that it burned whale oil, and that its fuel came from a shadowed spot high above, among the whale's ribs, which dripped slow, steady drops of oil, one every few minutes, into the lamp.

'Interesting,' Raven said. 'Why mustn't I touch it?'

'The lamp is the flame whose warmth holds the delicate balance between the whale's life and death,' said the girl, 'and if it were disturbed in any way it would be very dangerous for the whale, and for you as well.'

Raven nodded, and assured her he would not touch the lamp. Then the girl moved away, out of the light of the lamp, and disappeared from Raven's sight. As soon as she was gone Raven went over to the lamp and put out his hand curiously, catching the next slow drop of oil that fell. Then he licked it. It was sweet and good. He had always liked the taste of whale oil and whale meat. But then the girl returned, her arms laden with large fresh fish. That sight, with the flavour of the oil still lingering in his mouth, made Raven feel as if he had not eaten for a month.

He sat down with the girl and gobbled all the fish, and she watched him, smiling. 'You see there is plenty,' she said, 'even for your hunger.'

'So there is,' Raven agreed. 'And indeed I will stay with you a while.'

For the next few turnings of the tide Raven stayed with the girl-spirit, and ate the fish she gathered for him. And each time when she was gone to get the fish Raven put out his hand to catch drops of the oil and licked at them greedily. When he was not eating he sat with the girl and told her about all the many adventures he had had up and down the length of his days. She in turn told him of her quiet life within the whale, listening to the great steady heart-beat, and of the unbearable cold of northern waters or the pungent warmth of southern seas, and the strange fish and curious pieces of the world that the whale sometimes swallowed.

But after several days of eating fish and talking Raven began to grow bored, for there was not a great variety of things to do inside a whale. His thoughts turned increasingly to the delicious whale oil dripping into the lamp, drop by tempting drop. He had promised the girl-spirit that he would not touch the lamp, and each time she left to gather fish for him she made him repeat the promise. But always, as soon as she had gone, Raven would catch a few drops of oil and lick them up.

One drop at a time, though, was not enough. The oil only called up the wrinkles of hunger, it could not ease them. Nor could the fish, no matter how many he ate, ease his maddening hunger for the whale oil.

The next time the girl left him alone, Raven went over to the lamp and gazed upwards at the huge ribs, the wall of flesh behind them and the veins and capillaries, thick as logs, that ran along it. Perhaps, he thought, he could speed up the dripping of the oil if he could alter the special place in the flesh from which the slow drops fell. After all, he had promised not to touch the lamp, but had said nothing about touching the source of its oil.

He flew up easily to where the flesh curved above the lamp, and watched for a while as, at that one spot, the drops of oil formed and fell, as water gathers and drips from the stone ceiling of a cave. He reached out to touch the spot; the oil dripped on to his hand and he licked it off. But there was no change in the rate of the dripping. Reaching out again, he clawed at the spot lightly, and a small cut appeared in the flesh.

At the same time a faint shudder ran through the body of the whale. But Raven did not notice, for he had been elated to find that the slight cut had seemed to speed up the forming of the oil drops. He caught the trickle of oil in his cupped hands and drank the small pool that formed there, but still it was not enough. He wanted more and more of the sweet oil; his stomach clenched tight with his rising hunger. He put his face under the place where the drops formed and let the oil trickle directly into his open mouth.

Below, the lamp became starved of its fuel and began to burn low. As the flame flickered and weakened, the same powerful shudder passed through the body of the whale. But again Raven paid no attention, gulping mouthful after mouthful of the delicious oil.

Then the lamp went out.

What had been a shudder through the whale's body now became a terrifying convulsion. Raven was flung to one side, then to the other, then up and down, tossed about like a fir-cone in a whirlwind. The spine and ribs of the whale arched and flexed, the enormous body twisted, rolled, leaped through the air, bent in the middle. . . . Hour after hour the contortions of the whale went on, until Raven was nearly battered senseless within its body.

But finally the terrible storm of heavings and rollings began to quieten. And soon the whale came entirely to rest, and Raven lay in silence, stillness, and total darkness. Slowly he gathered his senses, and rose.

'Where are you?' he called to the girl-spirit. But not even an echo came back to him from the cavernous black depths around him.

'Where are you?' he called again. 'Come and help me!'

But the stillness remained unbroken. The girl was gone.

Taking out his fire sticks, Raven crept about in the darkness, hoping to find the lamp and make a flame. Perhaps, he thought, it would be possible to re-light the lamp and restore the life of the whale, and so bring back the girl. At the very least, with a flame he could see around himself. But searching in the scattered pools of oil he came upon only a few small fragments of what had once been the lamp. It was shattered beyond repair. The whale was dead.

Then Raven realised that he could no longer feel the wash of the sea, acting on the whale's body. Instead, his feet felt an earth's solidness beneath them. Clearly, in the last throes of its dying the whale had gone near to land, and now the waves had carried its body up on to a beach.

For a moment Raven felt saddened that his hunger had caused the whale's death, and caused its lovely spirit to depart for the faraway lands of the dead. But, even so, he remembered that he had set out in the first place to catch a whale for food. Now he had one, and even had it on a beach, where it would provide him with a great many large meals for some time to come. Indeed, he thought, he could start his first meal right then, and eat his way out of the whale.

But before he could begin, he felt the whale's body sway slightly — and, faintly, he heard the voices of men from outside. He knew what had happened: some humans living near the beach had found the whale, and were climbing over it, cutting pieces off for their own food.

Raven muttered angrily as he listened to the human beings carving pieces from *his* whale. Then all grew silent outside, and Raven guessed that the humans had carried their whale meat back to their village. Quickly he began clawing and hacking at the flesh of the whale from the inside, wanting desperately to cut his way out and, somehow, to carry off all the rest of the meat to a safe hiding-place before the human beings returned.

Soon he had tunnelled a way through flesh and blubber and skin, but he had barely reached the outside when he heard the lively chatter of the humans, hurrying back for more of the wonderful meat that had been given to them by the sea. There was no time for Raven to take more than a mouthful of blubber for himself. But then an idea came to him — and, before the humans came into view, he took his fire sticks and slipped them into the hole through which he had come, letting them drop back down into the belly of the whale.

Then the humans had reached the whale, and were staring up at him. 'Look, it is Raven on the whale's back!' a woman said, and there was much whispering and nudging among them.

Raven heard one old man say, 'What does that greedy one want with our whale?' but that voice was quickly shushed into silence, and then the chief stepped forward.

'Greetings, Raven,' he said. 'Have you come to see the great gift that the sea has brought to our village?'

'Yes, indeed,' Raven said, trying to appear kindly. 'And I have come to help you to gather the whale meat before it spoils.'

'That is very good of you,' said the chief. 'Now let us get to work.'

So, delighted to have Raven working with them, the human beings flung themselves into the labour of cutting up the whale. Under Raven's direction, they cut a huge swathe of whale skin and laid it on the beach, then piled on to it the huge chunks of meat that they were cutting from the body. 'In that way,' Raven told them, 'you can take all the meat back to the village at once, without having to make several trips.'

They worked hard, and the pile of meat grew and grew. Raven watched it with pleasure, and watched also some of the humans begin to cut their way into the interior of the whale. Soon the cry went up for which he had been waiting.

'Look! Fire sticks! There are fire sticks here in the belly of the whale!'

The villagers crowded round, muttering with astonishment at such a strange thing. Raven crowded up with them.

'Fire sticks in the whale?' he said. 'That is bad — a very bad omen!'

The villagers nearby turned to stare at him nervously.

91

'What is the bad omen, Raven?' asked the chief.

'The omen says . . . but then I don't want to frighten you,' Raven said. 'After all, it may not be true.'

'Tell us, tell us!' the villagers cried.

'Very well — the omen says, as I have heard it, that when fire sticks are found in the belly of a whale, anyone who has taken meat from that whale will die!'

The crowd gasped, and began to back away from the whale. Many who were still holding portions of whale meat quickly dropped them.

'But what is it that will cause these deaths?' asked the chief.

'I do not know, and I do not want to stay to find out,' Raven cried. 'I am leaving this place as fast as I can, and leaving the whale meat behind!'

And he sprang into the air and flew away, as high and as fast as he could.

But very shortly he swung back in a great arc towards the whale. And, just as he expected, he saw the human beings stampeding away like a herd of terrified caribou back towards their village.

Raven swept down and landed beside the huge pile of meat which, at his bidding, the villagers had so neatly and carefully laid down. He rescued his fire sticks from the whale, but for a while he was unable to make a flame because he was laughing too hard. Soon though, he had a fire burning, and a large piece of whale meat and blubber roasting over it.

Not one of the villagers dared to come down to that beach again until long after Raven had gone from there, leaving behind only the enormous and well-cleaned bones of the whale.

10

Coyote and the Acorns
YOROK

ONE day after the first forests had reached their full growth, Coyote's keen nose became aware of a most delicious smell.

It was something he had never smelled before, and it had him pawing the ground in hunger. Raising his nose high so he would not lose the smell, he sped through the forest, back-tracking the breeze that had borne the smell to him. It led him to a village of human beings.

The humans made Coyote welcome, as they always made any of the People welcome. The men gathered round him, asking friendly questions about his doings and his wanderings, inviting him to join their circle and smoke a pipe with them. The children tugged at him, to make him come and play with them or tell them a story. Coyote smiled and nodded at them all, but still his nostrils were filled with the wonderful smell, and he could neither join the men's circle nor run off with the children. Instead, he made his way over to the cook-fires where the women were.

One of the women was wrapping leaves round a soft, flat thing that looked like a thin cake. 'What is that,' Coyote asked her, 'that is making this beautiful smell?'

'This is what we call sour acorns,' she said. 'Would you like some?'

'Yes, very much,' said Coyote, his mouth watering so that the slaver spilled down his chin in rivulets.

'Join us, then,' said the woman. 'There is plenty for everyone. We are ready to eat now.'

So Coyote sat down with the villagers, and impatiently watched the women scrape the cook-fires aside with green sticks and uncover the hot, leaf-wrapped acorn cakes. One

95

of the cakes was placed before Coyote, and the smell of it made him forget his manners, and even forget the cake's blazing hotness. He swallowed the whole in one gulp. The village women smiled and brought him another, and he gulped that one down the same way. Soon Coyote had eaten twenty-four of the cakes, and would have eaten more, except that there were no more ready for cooking.

'How do you prepare this miraculous food?' Coyote asked the woman who had served him.

The woman was delighted that he had enjoyed his meal so much, and flattered that he should be interested in how it was cooked.

'Why, it is something anyone can do,' she said. 'You soak the acorns in water, press them down hard, and leave them pressed for two days. Then you simply wrap them in leaves and bake them under the coals of a fire.'

Coyote looked at the woman for a long moment. Then he smiled and shook his head. 'Come now,' he said. 'There must be more to it than that. Nothing so delicious as this food could be so simple to prepare.'

'But it is,' the woman assured him. 'Just that simple.'

Coyote still shook his head.

'Perhaps the recipe is a secret. Never mind, you can trust me not to give the secret away. You can tell me how to make your sour acorns.'

'But she has told you,' said one of the other women. 'Soak the acorns, press them and cook them. There is nothing more.'

Coyote looked around at them in exasperation. 'I don't know why you should lie to me. Have I not always been your friend? Why can you not tell me the truth about sour acorns?'

'Please believe us, friend Coyote,' pleaded the women. 'It is as we have told you. Why do you think we are lying?'

'I *know* you are lying,' snapped Coyote, 'because nothing that tastes so good could be made so easily. It is against the way of things.'

'But, Coyote. . .!' the women began.

'Do you take me for some short-sighted, thick-brained fool without smell or sense?' shouted Coyote. 'There must be more to the cooking of acorns than you have told me, and I want to know the rest of it!'

The women looked at each other, bewildered, not knowing what to say. Then one of the old grandmothers came slowly forward.

'You are quite right, friend Coyote,' said the old woman. 'Good things must always be difficult to come by, as you say. So we will tell you the true way to prepare sour acorns, won't we, sisters?'

And she turned to the other women and gave them a broad wink that Coyote could not see.

'Now first,' the old woman went on, turning back to Coyote, 'you must gather only the biggest and whitest acorns. The smaller, ordinary ones, with a taint of green at the end, will not do. When you have gathered enough acorns, you must load them in a canoe and paddle it to the middle of a large river. There you must tip the canoe over, so that the acorns will be drowned.'

'Drowned,' repeated Coyote, listening closely and nodding his head to show that he understood.

'Once the acorns are drowned,' said the old woman, 'you must then search for two flat stones, as perfectly smooth as river ice, to use in pressing the acorns. And when you have found them, you must gather special firewood — only the dried branches of the blackthorn. These you must peel and then scrape down so that only the central pith remains.'

'The pith,' repeated Coyote, nodding harder than ever.

'Finally,' continued the old woman, 'the pressed acorns must be wrapped only in the leaves of the poison sumac. Any other leaves will not give them their special flavour.'

'Drowning, blackthorn pith, sumac leaves,' repeated

97

Coyote happily. 'I will remember. I knew the dish would have to be complicated, to be so good. You might have told me the whole recipe in the first place.'

And off he raced to begin his preparations, muttering to himself the recipe that the old woman had given him. He was concentrating so hard on remembering it all that he did not hear the wave of giggling that spread among the women of the village behind him.

Coyote spent a long time selecting his acorns. He threw aside any that he thought were small, or unevenly shaped, or even faintly tinged with green at the stem. It took him several days, but finally he had enough to load into his canoe, placing them in gently, handful by handful, so as not to bruise them.

Then he carefully pushed off from the shore of the great river where his canoe was moored, and paddled out to the centre. As he felt the fierce current clutch the canoe, he took a deep breath and flung himself sideways. The canoe overturned, plunging Coyote and all the acorns into the freezing water. At the same time, the descending edge of the canoe struck Coyote a sharp blow on the head. He spluttered to the surface, then swam dazedly to shore.

There, soaked, chilled, and with aching head, he began looking for the smooth, flat stones he needed. Again the search took a long time, for he threw aside any that showed even a faint roughness or bumpiness. But within a few days he had found his stones. He also had stubbed toes, cracked shins, broken nails, and a soreness still from the bump on his head.

Next, Coyote went into the woods to look for blackthorn trees. When he found them, he took nearly a day to break off the dry branches that he needed, and several days more to scrape and hack away the wood down to the pith. As he worked the thorns scratched and stabbed him, and many stuck so deep into his flesh that no amount of picking could dislodge them.

98

Lastly, Coyote looked for poison sumac leaves. When he found a stand of sumac, the picking went more quickly than the other tasks, because Coyote wanted to get through as fast as he could, and touch the leaves as little as possible. Even so, as he picked, he was giving low howls of pain as his flesh reddened, and swelled, and blistered.

But in the end the leaves were piled beside the stones and the pith, and Coyote was ready to cook his acorns.

At that moment a thought came to him.

'How generous those villagers were,' he said to himself, 'to let me eat twenty-four of their acorn cakes, when they must go through this much hardship and pain to prepare them!'

The thought made Coyote a little uneasy, and as he made his way down to the river where he had drowned his acorns, he began to feel even more worried.

'That old woman,' he thought, standing on the river-bank, 'did not tell me how to get my acorns out of the river, after drowning them.'

He started to run, as fast as his sore and aching body could go, along the river-bank. But no matter how far he went, in either direction, he found no acorns washed up. 'If they are drowned,' he thought, 'they will be at the bottom of the river.' And so he threw himself into the icy water, diving as deeply as he could. But the acorns had been carried off, long since, by the powerful current. Coyote saw only the smooth sand of the river-bed and a few inquiring fish.

Crawling back on to dry land, Coyote lay panting, trying to remember every word the old woman in the village had said to him. Surely, he thought, she *had* told him how to get his acorns back from the river, and he had simply forgotten.

He got slowly to his feet and stumbled away from the river into the forest nearby. There he came upon a group of women gathering acorns. They were not the women who had given him sour acorns, before, but were from another village. And Coyote noticed that they did not choose their acorns at all as carefully as he had, but picked up all sizes, whether they were green-tinged or not, as long as they were whole and not rotten.

Coyote painfully approached one of the women. 'Good day,' he said. 'I see you are gathering acorns. Will you be using them to make the dish called sour acorns?'

'Yes, indeed,' said the woman, straightening up from her work. 'Will you come, friend Coyote, and eat with us when the acorns are ready?'

'Perhaps,' said Coyote shakily. 'But first, tell me, how do you prepare that dish?'

The woman smiled. 'Nothing could be easier. Just soak the acorns, press them hard for two days, wrap them in leaves and bake them under the coals of the cook-fire.'

So Coyote knew that he had been a fool, and threw back his head to howl out his misery and pain.

Raven and the Fisherman

NORTH PACIFIC COAST

In the early times when all the world's parts had not been finally put in order, the human beings who lived by the side of the sea were always hungry. They could sometimes catch land animals and birds to eat, and in the right season they could pick salal berries and dig lily roots. But the rocky land alone could not provide enough to keep their bellies full and their children fat — especially during the harshness of winter when snow lay about them like a frozen desert. Yet they could find no food elsewhere, for in those times the fish of the sea stayed far away from the shore, farther even than the most fearless man would dare to go in a dugout canoe.

One cold, stormy day Raven flew along the coast-line and saw the humans huddling in their lodges, choking on the smoke that the wind blew back down the smoke-holes. He saw that the humans were thin and tired, that the children's ribs showed, that their skin was as slack on their bodies as that of the mountain bear in the spring after hibernation. And because Raven, who was the greediest of all the People, sympathized so much with the humans in their hunger, he made up his mind to help them.

'They would have plenty to eat,' he said to himself, 'if the fish of the sea could be made to swim closer to land. I have long wondered why they do not do so — now would seem a good time to find out.'

So Raven turned and flew out to sea, paying no attention to the buffeting wind and the splinters of cold spray from the wave-tops. After flying a long time, so that the land faded and vanished in the rain-mist behind him, he saw a very curious thing floating on the threshing waves beneath him. It was a large and sturdily built lodge, bigger and finer than the best lodge of the most important chief of any human beings on the land.

'A fine place like that,' Raven thought, immediately thinking of his stomach, 'ought to be able to provide delicious things to eat for a hungry traveller.'

So he swooped down and flew in through the smoke-hole of the lodge. And there, all alone, was a man sitting in an ordinary fashion by a fire. He was a strange man — hairless, with a pointed face, dressed in clothing that glistened in the firelight almost like the scales of a fish. The man seemed not at all surprised at Raven's arrival, but stood up and greeted him, and then asked who he was.

'I am Raven,' said Raven. 'Surely you know of me. Everyone knows Raven.'

'I am one who does not,' said the strange man. 'But I know only of things on the sea, and you are clearly not a sea creature.'

'I am of the sea, or the land, or the air, or wherever I wish to be,' Raven said. 'But who or what are you?'

'I have no name,' said the strange one. 'I have no father and mother, no sister or brother, no son or daughter. I live alone in this lodge on the tossing sea, and I have been here since the beginning of things.'

'If you live always on the sea,' said Raven, 'what do you find to eat?'

The man pointed to the sea beyond the door of his lodge. 'All the fish in the sea are there, at my bidding.'

And as if to prove it, he flung a fishing-line out of the door. In an instant it had tightened, and the strange man drew it in, with a huge halibut on the end. Raven's mouth watered as the man cooked the fish over the fire, and when it was done Raven gobbled his portion even more quickly than usual, because it was so meaty and delicious.

When their meal was done, the strange man took the remaining scraps and flung them out of the door into the sea. Raven blinked with astonishment, for as the scraps struck the water they had changed into a cluster of tiny fish.

'You are certainly the greatest fisherman I have ever met,' Raven said wonderingly. 'Not only can you catch a halibut in an instant, but you have all the fish of the sea waiting beside your lodge to be caught — and you seem to put more fish back in the sea every time you catch one.'

The fisherman nodded. 'That is why the sea is ever more rich with fish of all kinds, for I have been here since the sea first came to be.'

'Then why,' Raven asked, 'do you not move your house closer to the land, so that the human beings who live on the shore can harvest a few of these fish, and never go hungry again? You would never miss the few fish they would take.'

'I know nothing of human beings on the shore,' the fisherman said, 'and I care nothing if they are hungry or not. I am a being of the sea, and I and my fish will stay here, where the sea is deepest, far away from the edge of the land.'

Raven saw that there was no use arguing. Finally he asked, 'Do you not find that you grow lonely out here with nothing but waves and fish to keep you company?'

'I have never felt that way before,' the fisherman said. 'But since you have come to my house, and shared a meal with me, and talked with me, I think I may feel lonely if you leave. Would you not stay with me, Raven, here in my fine house, where you will never lack enough to eat?'

That was exactly what Raven had wanted him to say. 'Yes, fisherman,' he agreed, 'I will stay with you.'

So for many days Raven stayed in the lodge of the strange fisherman. When they were not eating they sat comfortably before the fire, talking.

Raven spoke of the world of land, describing the colours of the bluejay, the red cardinal and the snow goose, telling of the thickness of a grizzly's neck and of his temper, of the wolf's love of family, of how eagles built their nests among the clouds and how the wind sounded soughing through trees, unlike the wind upon the sea. The fisherman, for his part, spoke of the many faces of the sea, of the colour and variety of his own world. He described the speed and humour of the dolphin, told of the dark passage of the whale, silent in its depth, and of the bright shreds of colour that were the small fish of warmer seas.

But after a time Raven did not enter into the long conversations. Instead he sat gloomily and stared at the fire, or stared out of the door far across the sea, and gave deep, sad sighs, until at last — as he expected — the fisherman asked what his trouble was.

'Far away from here my father lives,' Raven explained craftily, 'in a lodge much like this one, floating on the sea. I have not seen my father for a long time, and I miss him very much.'

Then the fisherman sighed too. 'I have no father or mother, sisters or brothers, sons or daughters — but if I had a father, I would feel just as you do. I do not mind if you wish to leave me and go to see your father.'

'But why do you not come with me?' Raven asked.

'How?' asked the fisherman. 'I cannot fly, and this lodge moves so slowly over the water that I fear it would take forever for us both to find your father.'

In answer Raven gently lifted the fisherman off the floor, spreading his wings, and flew easily up to the ceiling of the lodge.

'We will travel like this,' Raven said. 'And I will take a pebble with us, which I can drop and change into an island, so that we can stop when we get tired and hungry.'

The fisherman agreed, and Raven carried him out through the smoke-hole, where they were flung high into the sky by the edge of a bitter east wind. Raven flew steadily out to sea — though of course he had no father to seek, and there was nothing out there but the grey waves reaching to the horizon. But even when his wings grew weary and his belly knotted with hunger he flew on, saying nothing.

Finally the fisherman spoke in a faint voice. 'I hope we find your father's lodge soon. I am cold and hungry, and I am a little afraid of being up so high.'

'Then we will stop and rest,' answered Raven, and dropped the pebble he had brought, circling in the sky above it. As the pebble struck the water it cracked open and grew wide and thick, until at last a small rocky island lay below, where before only the unbroken waves had heaved.

'Wonderful!' cried the fisherman. 'Now let us go down.'

'No, fisherman,' Raven said, 'only you will go down.' Swooping low over the sea near the island, he dropped the fisherman into the water.

'There is your new home!' he shouted to the fisherman. 'Swim for it!'

As he wheeled and rose in the air, he had a glimpse of the fisherman gliding through the water even more easily, it seemed, than a seal — and again the light glinted from his clothes, making them look like the scales of a fish.

He had every intention, on his return to the fisherman's lodge, of moving it closer to the land, so that all the fish which swarmed around it could be caught by the starving human beings. But when he reached the lodge, he remembered how easy it had been to catch fish there, and he decided to have something to eat before he began the work of moving the lodge.

Soon he had a fishing-line out of the door, and when he had gathered an immense heap of fish, he cooked them carefully over the fire. He was just swallowing the last bite, with his belly plump and round from the amount of fish he had eaten, when he heard a faint slithery splash from the doorway behind him. He turned in time to see the dripping body of the fisherman leaping towards him.

Too full to move quickly, Raven was flung to the floor,

107

and a pair of powerful, fish-cold hands clutched at his throat. 'Betrayer!' the fisherman hissed. 'You were going to steal my lodge! You did not know that I could swim as well and as fast as any fish, did you?'

Raven recovered himself and exerted his strength, hurling his attacker aside without difficulty, and rising angrily. 'I was not stealing your lodge!' he shouted. 'I was going to take it near the land, where the humans are starving!'

'I care nothing for your humans,' spat the fisherman, 'and I care nothing for you. Leave this lodge now, and do not return.'

So Raven, furious that his plan had been thwarted, flung himself out of the door and into the air, where he circled, thinking, and glaring down at the lodge which rose and fell away regularly on the steep waves beneath it. The wind remained strong, lashing the sea, and as Raven's great wings rode the wind easily, another idea came to him.

'Very well,' he said aloud, 'if the fisherman will not leave his lodge, I will take him with it to the humans on the shore!'

Down he flew and settled on the roof of the lodge. There he took a powerful grip on the sturdy roof poles and spread his wings to the fullest. Instantly the wind took them, filling them, swelling them like two great black storm clouds — and slowly, sluggishly, the lodge began to move. Soon it was gathering speed, drifting in the direction to which Raven's wings guided it, towards the land hidden by the far-off eastern horizon.

The closer he got to the shore, the more perversely did the wind blow. Raven's wings were torn at from all sides until he expected his finger feathers to be plucked out by its force, while his grip on the lodge roof dragged him down so that it felt as if his body would be pulled apart. Then, just when he thought he would have to release his grip, the fisherman sat up abruptly, suddenly aware that the lodge had been moving quickly forward for some time. Raven saw the flicker of the fisherman's silvery clothing as he dived out of the door of his lodge to see what was happening.

Instantly the fisherman saw Raven on his roof, and knew what was happening. He shouted, and shook his fist, and leaped high out of the water in his rage. But he could not get to the roof. And the fisherman's rage, all in vain, gave Raven new strength. He smiled grimly, and tightened his painful grip firmly once again, and the lodge sailed briskly onwards.

After what seemed to the exhausted Raven a journey of many more days, the land loomed suddenly into sight out of the mist. Raven lowered his wings thankfully, and the house drifted more slowly towards the shore until it came to rest, riding the waves no farther from the land than any canoe might safely travel. Raven gazed about him and saw that many human beings had come down to the sea's edge to stare at the remarkable floating lodge. Some of them seemed already to be making canoes ready to paddle out for a closer look, so Raven called to them in a ringing voice.

'This is the lodge of a fisherman who holds power over the fish of the sea!' he said. 'I have brought it to you so that the fish will stay near the land, to be food for you and your hungry families! But now stay on the shore — for I am going to end the power of the fisherman forever!'

As the humans watched fearfully, and as the fisherman raged from within his lodge, Raven stretched to his full height on the lodge roof, and spread one wing. The humans shrank down to their knees as a sudden great wind swept over them and out towards Raven, catching the wing and spinning it as though it were a flighted tree-seed. And as Raven turned, so too did the lodge. Slowly to begin with, then faster and faster, gaining momentum as the sea began to lose battle with its own laws and started to obey the law of Raven. Faster and faster the lodge spun so that the watching humans could see only a strange blur — and then they began to hear the terrifying roar of wind and sea,

109

screaming together around the lodge, drawn into the spin, forming a mighty whirlpool that deepened and widened as the noise rose and the spin became a great spout mounting the sky. As the spout swung into the sky, the sea seemed to open and widen into a great, black hole. Slowly, slowly the lodge disappeared from sight, and as the whirlpool quietened and the lodge disappeared, the water spout sank back down into the sea and Raven sprang out from its midst with a cry of triumph.

Then, as the foaming water closed over the lodge, there came from the rings of the disappearing whirlpool fountains of fish — halibut, cod, salmon, every kind of fish and shell-fish gushed out into the rapidly calming water, in more abundance than had ever before been seen at the edge of the land.

It may be that the silver-clad man who swam like a fish still lives in his fine lodge although it went to the bottom of the sea long ago: no one knows, and Raven never went to look. Certainly, though, there has never been a shortage of fish since the day that Raven brought them closer to land so that the shore-dwelling humans should never know hunger again.

Coyote in the Land of the Dead

YAKIMA

Eᴀʀʟʏ in the life of the world, Coyote paid a visit to the house of Eagle. There he found the cooking fire cold and untended and Eagle sitting at his door, rumpled and miserable.

'Eagle, what has troubled you so?' Coyote asked.

'Death,' Eagle said mournfully. 'My wife who has been with me from the beginning of things has died, and I cannot live my life without her.'

Coyote sat with Eagle then and thought about death. Wherever he went in the world, some being was grieving over the death of some other. Among the People or among humans, always there was the keening of women for their lost husbands or children, the tears of men for dead wives or babies, the lonely weeping of sons and daughters for the loss of parents. Coyote thought about all this sadness and despair, and made up his mind that the order of things should be changed.

'When winter comes,' he said to Eagle, 'leaves die and fall, flowers are eaten by the frost. But with the spring new leaves bud, new flowers sprout. It should be this way with all living things.'

'If only it were,' Eagle said.

'Very well then,' Coyote replied. 'In spring, when the buds are tight upon the boughs, we shall journey to the land of the dead — and we shall bring them back with us, so that the dead can rise each year when the world renews itself.'

Eagle leaped up. 'Why must we wait till spring?' he cried. 'Why must I endure my loss so long? Let us go now to bring back the dead.'

So Coyote and Eagle set off together, towards the west,

113

travelling by day and by night, through many sunrises and sunsets, stopping only when the nights were so dark that not one star glimmer could be seen. On those deep black nights they lay and listened to the murmurs of the spirits of the newly dead, passing like wisps of wind towards the same destination.

Finally, as they journeyed farther from places where humans or People lived, they entered a grey, flat land on which the sun seldom shone. And there, when the day was darkening with the onset of dusk, they came to the edge of the vast dark river that divides the land of the living from the land of the dead.

They gazed across the expanse of slow-moving water and saw that, in the shadowed distance on the far shore, there stood a village much like any other village, with smoke from cooking fires rising above the roofs of many lodges.

Coyote raised his voice and shouted across the water, calling for a boat to be sent for them. Eagle shouted as well, but their voices were swallowed up by the gathering twilight, and by the smoke-grey mist that clung to the river's surface. There was no sound from the distant village, nor could they see any movement.

'There must be no one there!' Eagle cried. 'How shall we cross?' And he called again and again to the silent lodges.

Then Coyote silenced him. 'They are there,' he said. 'But we must find another way to cross the river.'

He thought within himself for a while, and when the full blackness of night had closed in around them, he began to sing. It was a song he could not remember ever having heard, but at the same time it was a song he felt he had always known. The song rose and fell softly at first, but soon it carried across the river like thunder in summer heat. Not even the darkness or the thickening mists could smother it.

As he sang, out of the wide shadows on the water appeared four men in a black canoe, their paddles moving with the rhythm of Coyote's song. Yet their paddles did not quite seem to touch the water, while the canoe slid along the river's surface as if by itself. When the canoe touched shore, the four men sat silently, making no effort to help Coyote and Eagle as they climbed in. Then the canoe turned and slipped soundlessly back towards the shadowy far shore.

No splash of water sounded against the bows of the canoe or the blades of the paddles, and Eagle could not be sure whether the canoe floated on the water or on the mist, so silent was its movement. At one point Eagle tried to break the emptiness of the silence by questioning the four canoe-men about the village, and about his dead wife. But they paddled on without seeming to hear — except that they smiled gently to themselves, smiles that seemed to hold such depths of unearthly knowledge that Eagle shrank back from them, chilled.

Finally the canoe grated softly against solid earth and stopped. Again the four canoe-men sat motionless as Coyote and Eagle stepped out, the mists of the river-bank coiling round their feet, and set off towards the village.

At first they could not hurry, for the darkness in the land of the dead was so absolute that their eyes were no use to them. But then, ahead of them, a moon began to rise, pushing up into the sky as if the darkness clung to it and held it back. Its pale light showed Coyote and Eagle that they had at that moment arrived at the edge of the village. And there, waiting for them, stood a group of dark figures, silent and unmoving as the canoe-men had been.

As they drew closer, one of the silent figures stepped forward. It was an old woman, white-haired and wizened, but with a straight back and an eye as clear as a bird's.

'Why have you come to the land of the dead?' she demanded.

'We come on no harmful business, old woman,' said Coyote. 'But we have journeyed far, and we are cold and tired and hungry. Is there hospitality in this land, for travellers?'

The old woman nodded slowly. 'There is a place ready for you,' she said. 'But you must close your eyes and look at nothing around you. This is a sacred place, and what happens here in this village is not for the eyes of the living.'

So Coyote and Eagle closed their eyes, and were guided by wraith-light hands to the doorway of a lodge. Inside, they opened their eyes, and saw that the lodge was small but soundly built, of thick mats tightly woven from tule and other rushes, then bound together. There was nothing within the lodge but a heap of antelope hides to serve as sleeping places, and a small fire which gave off the heat of a very large fire, and did not smoke or seem to need fuel.

'I wonder if they will bring us food,' Eagle said.

'Perhaps when the night ends,' Coyote replied, 'when they have time for us.'

'Could we not go and search for food ourselves?' Eagle asked.

'See,' Coyote said. He pointed to the wall of the lodge where the doorway had been when they had entered. The wall was now smooth and unbroken, as were all the walls. There was no longer a way in or out.

Eagle looked around wildly. 'Then have we become prisoners of the dead? Can we ever leave?'

'Let us first try to see,' Coyote said, 'what happens at night in this village.'

He began picking at the rushes of the lodge wall with his nails, and Eagle came over and put his powerful talons to work. But every time they clawed out a small gap in the wall, it closed over before their eyes, as the doorway had done.

'It is no use,' Eagle said hopelessly.

Coyote thought for a moment. 'It must be because this is a lodge of the dead, which can be broken through only

116

by some implement from the land of the dead.'

'But we have none!' Eagle said.

'Perhaps we will find something,' Coyote replied.

As he spoke, the wall of tule mats beside them seemed to peel back like the gills of a salmon, and in the doorway stood one of the dark figures of the dead that had been with the old woman. He was carrying a large and beautifully carved wooden bowl, heaped with meat and steaming with delicious smells that brought the slaver to Coyote's mouth. He stepped in, and handed the bowl to Eagle and Coyote.

They gulped the food hungrily until nothing was left in the bowl but some clean-licked bones. Then Coyote took up the bones and crunched them to powder between his teeth before swallowing them. But when he came to the last bone he merely bit off a piece of it and chewed that up, keeping the rest of it hidden in his mouth.

When the silent food-bringer took back the empty bowl, Eagle asked him, 'When are we to be allowed out of this lodge? When can I seek my wife?'

But the dead one smiled that same gentle, sad, all-knowing smile that they had seen on the faces of the canoe-men, and said nothing, but turned and went out of the lodge. Behind him the doorway closed up to leave once more the blank, unbroken wall.

'They mean to keep us here forever!' Eagle raged. 'Until we are as dead as they are!'

'We shall see,' Coyote said, taking the sharp blade of bone from his mouth. He went to the wall and began scraping with great care at the tightly wound strands of tule. Slowly the bone cut its way through the mat, so that a tiny gap was made. As Coyote worked patiently on, the hole grew wider, and did not close over as the door had done.

Finally the gap was wide enough for both Coyote and Eagle to peer through at the same time. At first they could see little. The moon seemed barely able to force its thin light into the darkness of the village, so that the lodge

117

roofs were outlined while the ground around them was dense with shadow. Then, from what seemed to them the centre of the blackness outside, there rose the voice of a woman.

The voice began to sing, a beautiful song that reached deep into the hearts of Eagle and Coyote and awoke powerful feelings of both joy and sadness at the same time, stirring in them all the dreams and wishes they had never known, all the memories their lives had left them. Eagle recalled the beauty of his dead wife, and the first day he had met her, and laughed with pleasure at the memory, while in the same moment tears came to his eyes as he remembered her death. To Coyote the song brought a recollection of a day when he had felt especially powerful and had run the whole surface of the world, and another terrible day when the land was frozen and the ice would not melt. But though Eagle was wholly lost in the remembrances brought alive by the song, part of Coyote's mind was watching closely what was happening outside, in the village.

For as the song continued, the moon began to swell, and its light to grow brighter. Larger and larger it grew, until every part of the village and the open space in its centre could be seen more clearly even than by day, while only around the farther edges of the sky did night show a black seam.

When the moon had reached its brightest, the dead began to gather, from every part of the village, in the central clearing. They came dressed in rich ceremonial robes, splendidly decorated with shells and feathers. Some of them carried drums and musical instruments, and as they came all their voices took up the woman's song.

Coyote recognised many faces among the gathering, and then noticed one in particular, the lovely face of Eagle's wife. At that instant Eagle saw her too — but Coyote grasped him in a painful grip and silenced him just as he

118

was about to cry out.

'Be quiet!' he warned. 'They must not know we are watching!'

'But she is there, singing among the dead,' Eagle said, 'and she does not know I am here.'

'There will be time enough for her to know,' Coyote replied, 'when we take her and the others back among the living.'

'How are we going to take them?' Eagle demanded.

'You will see,' Coyote said.

Eagle watched Coyote go over to the heap of antelope hides and begin spreading them on the lodge floor. But though Eagle was curious, he was even more anxious to look again at his wife. So he turned back to the eyehole in the wall. Behind him, Coyote was hard at work.

He chipped off a needle-sharp splinter from the piece of bone he had kept, and then plucked out many of his own long, coarse hairs. With these he sat cross-legged on the floor and began sewing all the antelope hides together into an enormous bag.

When he was finally finished, he went over and peered through the eyehole. The moon was still shining as brightly on the ceremonials of the dead. The song still continued, and now the singers drifted and swayed in a dance like flames in a breeze, each of them smiling that sweet, sad, wise smile of the dead.

'Will you tell me now,' Eagle said, looking with surprise at the huge bag, 'how are we going to take the dead away from this land?'

'Wait,' Coyote told him again.

Then Coyote began to sing a song of his own. It was like the song he had sung at the river's edge, to summon the black canoe. His voice rose strongly above the voices of the dead, and smothered their singing like wet grass on a fire. As that song faded and Coyote's grew stronger, the moon began to dwindle and grow dim. It shrank from a sky-filling

119

hugeness to the size of a shield, a stone, a thumb-nail, at last to a mere pinprick in the sky like the smallest, most distant star.

Coyote stopped his song. In the single beam of the shrunken moon the dead were no longer dancing, but stood motionless, their heads bowed, held by the power of song. Beyond them there was nothing but the heavy, impenetrable darkness.

Coyote worked rapidly to enlarge the hole in the wall with the sharp bone, and soon there was space enough for them to slip through, dragging the hide-bag with them.

'If we put them all in this bag,' Eagle said, 'how will we ever carry it away?'

Coyote said nothing but went over to the nearest of the motionless figures, a motherly-looking woman. Gently he lifted her up, then motioned to Eagle to take her. To Eagle's astonishment, it was as if Coyote had handed him one of his own feathers. The woman weighed nothing.

'The dead are spirits,' Coyote told him, 'and have no weight or substance. So we can put them all in the bag as they are now, and they will come to no harm while we carry them back to the land of the living.'

Quickly he and Eagle gathered up all the others, until finally the sack was filled — though it remained as light as if filled with cobwebs. At the last Eagle brought the spirit of his wife and placed her tenderly with the others.

'Have their minds gone from them too, just as their flesh has?' Eagle asked worriedly. 'Will my wife be like this among the living, as still and empty-eyed as she is now?'

'No, she will be as awake and alive as we are,' Coyote assured him. 'They have all been put into a sleep by the song I sang, but they will awaken when the day comes. So hurry. We must be across the river and in the land of the living before dawn.'

The single beam of the moon gave enough light for Eagle

120

and Coyote to see their way as they left the village. But much of the night had been used up, and the moon was lowering itself to the horizon. Finally it set completely, before they reached the river. Eyeless again in the total blackness, they moved slowly, haltingly, every moment bringing the morning nearer.

At last they came to the edge of the river, with the blackness still unbroken around them.

'How are we going to cross?' Eagle asked. 'We cannot call the canoe-men now.'

'We have gathered them up with the others,' said Coyote. 'But we will use their canoe. Wait.'

Eagle heard Coyote move away along the river-bank, then silence closed around him. Coyote had not told him why they needed to cross the river before the daylight came, but even so he scanned the darkness anxiously. Was there the narrowest edge of grey, or of a lighter blackness, in the distance?

Soon Coyote returned, towing the great black canoe along the river's edge. They stepped into the canoe, carefully placing the bag in its centre, then kneeling and taking up their paddles, with Eagle at the bow of the canoe. No sooner had their paddles dipped towards the water than the canoe swung away from the shore.

Beyond them, in the east, a smear of grey had appeared on the edge of the sky.

'Why are we hurrying, Coyote?' Eagle asked. 'What will happen when the dawn comes?'

'The dead will awaken,' Coyote replied, 'from the sleep I put upon them in the village.'

'But we *want* them to awaken, in the land of the living!' Eagle said.

'Not so soon,' Coyote told him. 'When we cross the river the dead will come to life. They will no longer be spirits — they will have their solid bodies, their weight. Then in this bag they will be crushed together, unable to breathe. They

121

will be in pain, and afraid. Feel — already the canoe has grown heavier.'

It was true. Eagle could sense in the darkness that the canoe had begun to settle slightly on the surface of the river, even though it moved steadily on, at its own speed, without slowing.

'Then,' Eagle said, 'we must reach the land of the living and take them out of the bag before the day awakens them!'

'If we can,' Coyote said. 'But I think we are too late.'

The grey stain in the east had now spread farther up the sky as they talked. They thrust strongly with their paddles but, as before, the canoe of the dead moved neither faster nor slower. And now, faintly but more clearly every instant, they saw before them the looming far shore of the river, thrusting out of the darkness as the dawn reached down its fingers.

And the dead began to awaken.

From the bag there came muffled murmurings, at first no louder than breathing, then like the flutterings of flocks of birds. But soon separate sounds could be heard — a moan, the whimpers of children, a questioning cry, pained exclamations. And as the voices grew in strength so too the weight of the bag increased, and the bag moved and swayed as the cramped bodies within it struggled to ease their pain. The canoe also in turn tossed and swayed, its balance threatened, its lip dipping dangerously near the surface of the water.

'Be still!' Coyote suddenly shouted. His voice carried all the authority of his song, and for a long quiet moment the canoe skimmed on with neither movement nor sound from the bag.

Then it seemed that Coyote's command had broken the last link of the dead with their spirit-sleep. All their voices rose at once in a furious outcry. Now they were fully awake. Coyote and Eagle fought to hold the canoe upright, but in an instant the turmoil within the huge bag flung the canoe over on its side and hurled all its contents into the river.

Coyote swam quickly to the bag, lying like a small island on the river. Within it the dead still shrieked with pain and fear. Just as it began to settle deeper into the water, Coyote took hold of the hide bunched at its neck and began to tow it slowly towards the shore, now clearly outlined in the gathering light. Finally he reached the shallows of the river where Eagle swam up to join him. Together they lifted the bag's immense weight and stumbled up on to the land of the living.

Just as they did so, through the greyness of the eastern horizon, there appeared the first flare of the sun.

Coyote wrenched open the bag, and the shapes within it untangled themselves from the writhing cluster of arms and legs and crept one by one out into the light until at last all of them stood before Coyote and Eagle.

'We have brought you back to the land of the living,' Coyote told them. 'Now there will be no more death. All living things will return, as the trees and the flowers return, so that those who are left behind do not mourn, as Eagle has mourned his wife. Your spirits are clothed in flesh again, and you may go back to your villages and your homes.'

As he finished speaking, across the faces of his listeners crept the same quiet, wise smile that they had worn so often before. Then the white-haired old woman, who had spoken to Coyote and Eagle at the edge of the village of the dead, stepped forward to speak to them again.

'We understand your intentions, Coyote,' the old woman said. 'And we are glad to be remembered and still to be wanted among the living. But we have no wish to leave our land and return with you. We have known the sun and the summer, as you know it, and we have had our time there. But now we have also known the darkness and the winter

— and there is beauty and wonder and knowledge to be found there, too. In life there was much to do and much to learn; but in death there is the peace and stillness that allows one to find answers to greater questions, to gain wisdom even beyond your understanding, Coyote. Life is only one half of the time given to the spirit. Death is the other half, and by far the richer half — and we wish to return to it.'

She turned away, followed by all her people, to the edge of the river where the black canoe was waiting. Last of all went the wife of Eagle, and as she entered the canoe she turned to her husband.

'Do not grieve for me,' she said. 'We could never have returned to life. We are not the leaves of the tree, to die and be reborn, but like the tree's heart which must some day come to final death. But the tree is fed by the earth, which never changes, so that life and death are both part of its eternal rhythm and flow. And so are we. I cannot stay with you now, but someday you will cross this river again and then you will stay with me forever.'

So Coyote and Eagle watched in silence as the canoe glided away, back towards the land of the dead.